IT WAS JUST A COINCIDENCE

Albert Long

with

Chad Bonham

Hi Coach —

Your FCA friends wanted you to have this book. Enjoy!

Albert Long

COL. 3: 23-2T
PROV. 3. 5-6

Albert Long
One Marigold Place
Durham, NC 27705-1958
albertlong@frontier.com
(919) 309-1399

IT WAS JUST A COINCIDENCE

Cross Training Publishing
www.crosstrainingpublishing.com
(308) 293-3891

Cover Photo Credit: Photography by Steve Campbell,
steve@idovideophoto.com

A COINCIDENCE IS SOMETHING
THAT GOD ARRANGES,
BUT PREFERS TO REMAIN
ANONYMOUS.

To my wife, Jackie.
She is a real angel of mercy: The wind beneath the wings of our entire
family. She is my wife, my lover, my friend, my shoulder, and my strength.
Being, doing, sharing, understanding together for over 56 years.

"Coincidentally, I met Albert Long in the mid '60s when we were blessed to have him speak at McClenaghan High School in Florence, South Carolina. Wearing his University of North Carolina four-sport letter sweater, he was representing the Fellowship of Christian Athletes and speaking at our Character Emphasis Week program. I knew then from the tremendous positive influence he had on those students that he was the real deal. Coincidentally, Albert has been the real deal for our Master Coach to everyone he has ever met, and a dear friend of mine. This is a must read or you will miss an unbelievable opportunity to meet a man of God's own choosing! These inspiring accounts of "Happenings" in his life will be a great influence on your life!"

Fisher DeBerry
Former Head Football Coach, United States Air Force Academy

"It Was Just a Coincidence is not just Albert's FCA story, but a great historical read of the growth of FCA and the foundational builders of faith he met along the way. I traveled the path of my own FCA experience while reading and reliving my FCA life and true commitment to Christ at Black Mountain FCA camp. Once I began reading I did not want to stop, but looked to the next experience he shared. My heart was blessed. My time with Albert in FCA and Happenings, Inc., gave evidence of how the Lord changes hearts, direction in life, and gives a person a ministry to impact lives, and Heaven."

Dal Shealy
VP of FCA Football Coaches' Ministry and former FCA President

"It's no coincidence that I dribbled a basketball between Albert's legs years ago, which by the way, made him pretty mad at me! Now as brothers in Christ, we've formed a lasting friendship. We've spent time together, ministered together and prayed together. I've been entertained and blessed by his stories. I'm so glad he is putting them down on paper. I know you'll enjoy the book and appreciate his witness for Christ.

Bobby Richardson
Former Yankees All-Star and World Series Champion

"Albert Long has the ability to see the hand of God at work in every day events. He sees what other people don't see and recognizes it as part of the overall purpose of God. Albert knows that things do not happen by accident. Everything is a part of God's purpose. He cites many examples of God's intervention in his life and ministry. Every reader will resonate with these examples. He then goes a step further to show how this relates to Biblical passages and how it can be applied to the reader's life. The short one-sentence summaries capture the essence of great truths. Every reader's life will be greatly enriched by reading, studying, and applying *It Was Just A Coincidence*. The letter-sweater kid deserves another letter!"

John Ed Mathison
Founder of John Ed Mathison Leadership Ministries

"Meeting Albert Long means encountering his effervescent spirit, his boyish enthusiasm and his happy knack of making friends for life with all kinds of people in all kinds of places. That being the case, meeting him in the pages of his book about "coincidences" drawn from his lifelong habit of just being Albert will take you on a trip that will encourage you to check out your own coincidental life experiences and see if, like Albert you can see in them the hand of God at work. And if like Albert you are an aging jock, you will love the stories of his friendship with many of them!"

Stuart Briscoe
Author, broadcaster and speaker

"I first met Albert Long in 1972 when he conducted a Happenings rally at my high school in High Point. He was faithful to share the Gospel of Jesus Christ then and has been faithful to continue for over 50 years. Albert has ministered to more teenagers in North Carolina than anyone I know. I count it a privilege to have ministered with Albert for all these many years."

Johnny Evans
Fellowship of Christian Athletes, Eastern North Carolina Director

ACKNOWLEDGEMENTS

I'm certain I'll get myself in trouble for this simply because I know I'll leave someone out. For those that I do, you will know who you are, and please forgive me. There are many great friends of mine, or the ministry of Happenings, Inc., that I have not mentioned in the book.

To my dear friends Bobby Poss, John Walker and Barry St. Clair, that have not only been with me through many trials and tribulations but more good times than bad. To Mike Aldridge and Mike McCartney, two "Mike's" who have supported me and our little ministry that has always stood tall in the eyes of our great Lord, from the very beginning.

To Mike McCoy, John "Bull" Bramlett, Mickey Marvin, Jim Ritcher, Chuck Walker, Charles Waddell, Gary Cuozzo, Greg Brezina, Buddy Curry, Bill Curry, Don McCauley, Norm Evans, Sammy Johnson, Ken Hatfield, and Carrol Dale, who are all former NFL players and FCA supporters that have set examples for me these many, many years.

To all the college and NFL coaches that have been a pillow I could always lean my head on: Coach Sylvia Hatchell, Bob Lord, Steve Hagan, Bob Sanders, Clyde Christianson, Allen Williams, Tony Dungy, Moyer Smith, and I'm certain many more.

To Hank Parker, George Hamilton IV, Carl Erskine, Danny Buggs, Ken Johnson, Dr. J.L. Williams, Lake Speed, Aubrey Edwards and Bobby Clampett who have always shown me their support, especially by being on the Advisory Board of Happenings, Inc.

To my former Board members and Advisory Board members who are now "absent from the body and present with the Lord."

Board members: Lad Boyle, James "Slug" Claiborne, Pete Covington and Clyde King.

Advisory Board members: Paul Anderson, Pastor Bob Baggett, Ed Britton, Coach Nick Hyder, James Jeffrey, Charlie Justice, Coach Tom Landry, John Lotz, Grady Nutt, Don Shinnick, Rev. Calvin Thielman and Loren Young.

To my two college roommates Will Alexander and Bill Booth. I'll never forget Will reading his Bible every night before going to bed long before I became a real Christian, and I have to thank Bill for serving on the Board of Directors of Happenings, Inc., many years later.

To my pastor Stan Geyer, as well as all the Elders and Deacons at Springs of Life Bible Church and so many in our congregation. To all of you who are in our Thursday adult men's Bible Study in Chapel Hill which I live for each week. I thank all of you and appreciate your faith in the ministry to Danny Lotz and me these many years.

To Louis Alexander and Michael Dean Chadwick who were so loyal to John Lotz right up until the good Lord called him home, and who are still a blessing to me.

All of the above, plus many I'm certain I have left out, have always been gifts of God to me as well as treasures that all the money in the entire world could never buy. I thank you from the bottom of my heart.

FOREWORD

Everybody knows that Albert Long is a man who is full of divine appointments. It is who he is. I would suppose that I too met Albert by a strange coincidence. I had just hired Mark Dickerson as minister of music at my church. Mark and I met a Black Mountain, North Carolina, at an FCA event. When I interviewed him, he told me he did some work with a guy I had to meet. In fact, he thought he would be at Black Mountain while we were there and maybe I could talk to him about what they had done together.

My coincidence with Albert occurred while sitting in a historical white rocking chair on the front porch at Lee Hall. By the way, that's where Albert and I have spent a lot of hours together ever since that meeting. When we first met, I was thrilled to learn of Mark and Albert's "Happenings" ministry. Now when I think back to that divine appointment, I'm even more thrilled to know that in that moment I had met the man that would be a part of my faith journey for almost 35 years. He was a treasure from then on.

I would later begin an itinerant ministry of my own and I would almost mirror Albert's ministry. He wanted to impact kids and so did I. He connected to men through athletics and I wanted to do that as well. I suppose the meeting with Albert was one of God's divine appointments that would prepare me for my ministry of 30 years.

I have wondered what it was about Albert that drew me to him. Certainly it was the athletic background. He was a legend by the time I met him. His humility impressed me and his stories fascinated me. He had been impacting FCA for years and there I was to learn.

I am certain I was attracted by his humor. He wasn't the best joke teller in the world, but he still loved to try. It was a joy to take his horrible stories and use them in my own speaking.

I loved the way he related to people. His concern and desire to know who you were and where you had been was evident to each of us who met him.

I was also fascinated with the way Albert could communicate in so many ways with so many different types of folk. Kids loved him, adults fed off his words, and he has even mellowed out to be a good Bible teacher. There are rumors that he studies now and it is certainly obvious when you hear him teach.

Albert is a servant. I have watched him agonize with folks that were hurting and laugh with those who were laughing. I recall a time he was asked to speak at a funeral for an old friend and he worried about the best way to minister to the family as well as to those who would come. That servant attitude drew me to him.

Albert's journey of faith is appealing to me as well. He has not ceased to allow himself to stay in the journey. He continues to grow and I have enjoyed having him sit in my preaching sessions. He always makes eye contact with you while speaking and he's an encourager and a great friend all the time.

You are about to read some of that journey. The people mentioned in this book are deeply meshed in a relationship with Albert and have journeyed with him. Some of them are big names and some are not so big, but all of them have discovered the real reason Albert has so many friends. He is a reflection of Jesus.

Enjoy the book and enjoy the man. I think he is a treasure to read, to know and to experience through these many moments that were just a coincidence.

Ken Smth
An old preacher still preaching
Fellowship of Christian Athletes Hall of Champions recipient

INTRODUCTION

Me write a book? You've got to be kidding me! The only reason that subject came up two years ago was because so many people asked me why I never have written one. It made me think, so I decided to look into it. I called my friend Adam Lucas to see if he had time for me to buy his lunch. Adam is the editor of *Tar Heel Monthly* and has written over a dozen books.

Adam met with me and he listened to my ideas. He loved them, especially what the title of the book would be if it ever became a reality, and my "coincidence" story ideas. Then he asked me that one question I never thought of. He asked me where my audience would be. He mentioned that I was almost eighty years of age, was not speaking much at the present time, and if I could not get Fellowship of Christian Athletes (FCA) 100% behind it, then Jackie and I would have a lot of books just sitting in our garage.

At this point I knew this project would not be easy, but I also knew things would come together if the good Lord wanted me to do this.

I contacted a former UNC fraternity brother in New York, thoroughly explained my situation to him, and asked him if his foundation would consider funding this project if it worked out. He was very polite, and right to the point when he told me they funded medicine, education and the arts and nothing religious. I understood that this was a sign from God not to proceed at that time and I put the book idea on the back burner.

Then one early morning in March of 2012, about two years later, I awoke with this book idea on my mind once again. In my prayers I asked the good Lord what He was telling me. I wrestled with the idea for the next few days and decided to call my friend Dan Britton who was located in the FCA home office in Kansas City. Dan's dad, Ed Britton, was a dear friend of mine who served on the Advisory Board of my ministry Happenings, Inc.

Dan absolutely loved the idea, especially when I explained how the entire book would be lifting up our great Lord through my many FCA stories and "coincidences." Dan told me that FCA would most certainly promote it if it became a reality. He also suggested a writer and a publisher and offered to contact both of them for me. I asked him to please do so.

Now I saw my real problem. Where was the money going to come from for this endeavor? After much prayer, and I mean much prayer, I decided to do something that I really did not want to do. I pulled out my Happenings, Inc., mailing list, which consisted of approximately 750 people, and came up with the names of fourteen individuals. These were friends that I thought would be interested in this book idea and could easily afford to make a $1,000.00 investment into the ministry. My goal was to raise $10,000.

I wrote a letter to each of these fourteen individuals, explained my idea, and included a self-addressed post card with "count me in" in one block and "sorry, but I'll pray for this" in the other. I was overjoyed with the results as well as a real miracle that took place shortly afterwards.

A sister of one of the "count me in" supporters heard about the book from her brother, contacted me, and told me she wanted to be included. Three other people who heard about this by word of mouth also contacted me and offered their financial support. The only thing I could say was "thank you Lord." In a short period of time, there were commitments for $11,000 plus a "let me know what else you will need" from one of my dear former Board member friends.

By this time Chad Bonham and Gordon Thiessen, the writer and publisher Dan had recommended to me, were ready to go. All I could think about was how the hand of God had directed me in this endeavor.

I immediately started writing down every incident that had

happened to me over the years that friends told me were just a coincidence. I asked Chad to make certain that he provided my definition of coincidence in big bold print on the inside front page: "A coincidence is something that God arranges but prefers to remain anonymous."

Chad came to my Durham home and he taped and listened and taped and listened until he was ready to go back to Oklahoma. After two and a half days with him, I have been excited every day since and now this book is finally a reality. Was it a miracle from the very beginning? I think so! That's why I have always understood the truth found in Philippians 4:13.

*"I can do **all things through Christ** who strengthens me."*

CONTENTS

PART ONE

It was just a Coincidence
My Story

1963. That's when it all started. Of course, plenty had already happened up until then. I had enjoyed a four-sport career at Durham High School and then became the first four-sport letterman in Atlantic Coast Conference history during my playing days at the University of North Carolina. I also spent time in the Air Force, got married to a beautiful young lady I met my senior year at UNC, started a family, and was well on my way to becoming a successful insurance salesman.

But it wasn't until 1963 when my life *really* started.

That's when Ted Youngling, who was an assistant football coach at Duke University, called me and asked me to be program chairman for a citywide Fellowship of Christian Athletes program in Durham. I never realized that it would be the beginning of something so wonderful. Before that, the only part I had ever played for the organization was when I was invited to speak at two different UNC events by my close friend Danny Lotz.

Accepting the offer to be program chairman didn't change my life immediately, but it set my feet on a path that the good Lord had laid out for me. That was a journey that would take a few years to complete.

In the meantime, that FCA gathering was one of my first opportunities to build some new friendships. That's where I met Baltimore Colts linebacker Don Shinnick who was one of the special guests. I made sure to assign myself to host #66 for the duration of our three-day event.

Don found out that the Durham fire chief had one of his gospel tracts from when he played at UCLA and he wanted me to take him to meet the chief. I took Don to the station and almost got into big trouble. He was determined to go down the fire pole, which he did, and hit so hard at the bottom that he hurt his back. I could see the paper the next day: "Starting linebacker for Colts out for the season because of sliding down a fire pole." Thank goodness he was okay.

Despite that mishap, we stayed in touch and eventually Jackie and I became close friends with him and his wife Marsha. The first time I ever did my "Letta Sweatta" routine a few years later was at a high school assembly that Don arranged. He was in the audience and laughed harder than the students. I knew immediately that the monologue would probably be my future trademark, which it certainly was.

After the citywide program, Ted invited me for the fourth year in row to attend the FCA national conference at Henderson Harbor in New York. I had turned him down the previous three times, but he never gave up on me. I really wasn't too excited about it. I loved the word "fellowship" and I loved the word "athletes." And even though I was a good guy who attended church every Sunday, I didn't know how I felt about the word "Christian."

Because of Ted's persistence, I finally accepted the invitation and drove all the way to New York with John and Danny Lotz. Every time I've told this story since, I've always said that perseverance is what got the turtles to the Ark to illustrate how thankful I was that Ted never gave up on me.

My relationship with the Lotz brothers started back in 1956 when Danny came to Chapel Hill to play basketball for the Tar Heels. He was a member of the 1957 undefeated national championship team and later married Billy Graham's daughter Anne. John was a very successful high school coach on Long Island and would occasionally visit Danny. Two years after our trip to Henderson Harbor, he would join Dean Smith's staff at UNC. John would later become the head coach at Florida before returning to Chapel Hill to become an assistant athletic director.

From Durham To Henderson Harbor And Beyond

That long drive turned out to be more eventful than I could have ever imagined. It was the next to last night of the conference that I'll never forget. James Jeffrey (or Jeff, as we all called him) was the speaker and he was the best I'd ever heard at that time. Six months later, he would become the CEO of FCA due to Bob Stoddard's untimely death while playing handball.

But it wasn't just Jeff's talk that moved me. For four days and nights, I had been around people who never used profanity. I heard no dirty jokes. I heard no gossiping. It was unbelievable to me. Afterwards, I went up to Jeff and said, "Something is bothering me."

"I know what it is," he replied. "I've been watching you this week and I'm glad something has been bothering you. We're going to take care of that right now."

We went outside and Jeff told me to kneel down.

"Excuse me?" I said.

"Kneel down," he firmly repeated.

So I knelt down and he knelt down beside me. Then, he made an even stranger request.

"Take my hand."

"Excuse me?" I said.

"Take my hand and repeat after me," Jeff replied. "And concentrate on what I'm saying."

He prayed and I repeated and he prayed and I repeated and he prayed and I repeated. I got tired of hearing him pray because every time he said something, I had to repeat. When Jeff finally said "Amen," I looked up. I didn't see a burning bush. I didn't see shooting stars. But I remember one thing he said to me.

"Albert, congratulations. You're a brand new person."

When I got up the next morning, I shaved and looked in the mirror and said to myself, "That's me. I'm not a brand new person. What is this stuff he was talking about?"

Then I went to breakfast and a guy came up to me and hugged

me and said, "God bless you brother. I heard you were saved last night."

My answer to him was, "Sir, I'm not your brother. I don't know you. And I haven't been swimming since I've been on this island." That's what "brother" and "saved," meant to me at the time.

Even though I had been in church most of my life, the people at the conference spoke a different language. I didn't know what it meant to be someone's brother in Christ and I didn't know what it meant to be saved. And I was even more confused when they would say to me, "You've got to tell people what happened."

I kept thinking, "How can I tell people what happened when I don't *know* what happened?"

As much as I wanted to do as they said, I couldn't tell others about my experience at Henderson Harbor without making a fool out of myself because I had no idea what to say. That probably lasted about one month before I quit trying.

The next year, I went to the first ever FCA conference at Black Mountain and I got my battery recharged. Everything was fine for five days and then I came back home. I went up to people that I thought were Christians and I asked them to help me. They all told me "Don't do," "Don't do," "Don't do," "Don't do."

When I finally got to a person that I just knew was a professing Christian, he said, "Don't do this and don't do that and don't do this and don't do that and don't you ever, ever, ever think about doing *that!*"

At that point, I decided I would just go back to sinning. It was a whole lot more fun and a lot easier to understand. That was exactly how I felt. I was a baby lamb. I wanted these people to feed me. I wanted them to tell me what was going on. You don't put a baby lamb out to pasture. You feed it until it becomes a sheep. I was a baby lamb and I was being put out to pasture. No wonder I was so confused.

I didn't understand this at the time, but what that situation taught me was that religion without reality breeds rebellion. It's something that I have seen through the past 40 years of ministry on college campuses.

Religion is when someone shakes that Bible in your face. Religion teaches you that there's a God, but if you've never discovered this God, then this God might be a drag on what you want to do. Religion teaches you that there is a Jesus that died for you on a cross, but if you're not convinced, you won't understand why you should give your life to Him. That's what I went through.

Those first two years, I also kept hearing people tell me, "You've got to take that first step." But I didn't know what that meant. Walking assumes that you have a destination. Walking assumes dependency. And I did not have that. I didn't know where I was going and I wasn't dependent on the Lord.

In 1965, I was invited to speak to over 800 guys at Black Mountain. I was so excited to speak that night and I was good. I knew I was good because everybody told me I was good.

But there was one coach there who wasn't impressed. He walked up to me that night and put his finger on my nose. He said, "I've been watching you Long, and I just have one thing to say to you. I dare you to challenge the resurrection of Jesus Christ. But reject not until you've examined all the evidence."

I asked him to explain what he meant and this is how he responded:

"I dare you to challenge that stone. Challenge how that stone covered that tomb. Challenge how that stone was moved. Challenge every narrative that was ever written about the resurrected Christ. Every one of them says that the grave clothes remained undisturbed. I dare you to challenge the custodian, those elite soldiers that guarded that tomb.

"But most important, he continued, "I dare you to challenge all the appearances that our Lord made after He was resurrected. Then you will have to decide, 'Did He or didn't He?' And then you will have to do something about it when you realize that He did rise from dead and walk out of that tomb."

I was determined right then that I was going to find out what had happened to me at Henderson Harbor and those two trips to Black Mountain. So I had to get involved in a Bible study and I had to learn how to pray, when to pray, why to pray, where to pray and what to say. It all seemed impossible to me, but that's when God really got a hold of me.

Now, I've never heard Him speak audibly, but when you're saved and the Holy Spirit comes into your life, you'll understand what God wants you to know. And one night during that process, I felt as if He was speaking to me. This is a modern interpretation of how that conversation might have gone:

"Albert!"

"Is that You God?"

"It's Me. I just want to tell you, I'm proud of you."

"You should be God. Did you hear me at Black Mountain?"

"I sure did."

"Was I good?"

"One of the best I've ever heard."

"You mean that Lord?"

"I sure do."

"I'm making it Lord. It's not as hard as I thought it was going to be."

"No, you've got a long way to go, son."

"Wait a minute. What do you mean I've got a long way to go?"

"You've got to love Me with all your heart, soul, strength and mind. Did you hear Me? Not yourself. You've got to love *Me!*"

"I don't know how to do that. It might be impossible. How do I do that?"

"But there is a lot more," He replied. "You've got to love your enemy."

Now that one knocked me between the eyes, but I realize now that He was telling me that the only way I could conquer my enemy was to love him. That doesn't mean you have to associate with him, but you've got to love him. That means you've got to have good will toward your enemy. You place your enemy in God's hands for disposition and let Him handle it.

The conversation continued:

"Lord, it's impossible. I can't do these things."

"Albert, I've got someone who can get you through the impossibility and His name is Jesus Christ. You have most certainly met Him, but you don't know Him. You're never going to make progress until you get rid of self and accept Jesus Christ and get to know Him."

That's when I finally understood my situation. That's when I learned the two most misunderstood words in the Bible: "Believe on."

I went to the dictionary and looked up those two words. "Believe" means, "To accept trustfully on faith or "to adhere to." "Adhere" means, "To stick like glue." The word "on" means, "To make contact with."

So "Believe on" means to make contact with Jesus Christ and stick to Him like glue. That's every day of every week of every month of every year. From that moment on, I decided to yield my life to Him. All of a sudden, I didn't want to live in my old lifestyle anymore. I really understood what the indwelling of the Holy Spirit was all about. It was such an incredible time.

The Teen Crusade Years

By 1969, I was becoming more active as a featured speaker at sports banquets and FCA events. I was already friends with New York Yankees star second baseman Bobby Richardson, whom I first met in 1958 when he brought his traveling basketball team to play against the football players at Shaw Air Force Base. That was the game where Bobby famously dribbled between my legs.

Bobby introduced me to Reverend Sam Anderson who was the pastor of a small Presbyterian church in Kershaw, South Carolina. Sam had decided to start a ministry called Teen Crusade and enlisted Bobby to put a team together. Bobby brought in Billy Zeoli to be our evangelist. Billy was CEO of Gospel Films and had occasionally worked with Baseball Chapel for the Yankees.

Sam and Bobby asked me to lead the high school and middle school assemblies and serve as the emcee for our evening meetings. The rest of the team consisted of Lee Fisher, our song leader, his wife Betty who was in charge of counseling, recording artist Erv Lewis, and PGA golfer and Ryder Cup member Dave Ragan.

Dave was an especially interesting member of the team. He had accepted Christ not long before that while watching a Billy Graham Crusade on television. It was "just a coincidence" that Bobby Richardson was one of the guest speakers that night.

A little later on, we were blessed to add Lt. Clebe McClary. He was a U.S. Marine and Vietnam veteran. I'll never forget Clebe going with me to hear me speak at an assembly program in South Carolina. When it was over he said, "I hope some day I'll be able to do what I just heard you do." It didn't take long for Clebe to stick me in his hip pocket. He is still one of the most outstanding patriots in our country today—a real American. Clebe often talked to the young people about how he had lost his left eye and his left arm in Vietnam and how he became a Christian during a Teen Crusade event in Florence, SC after the war.

One of our first Teen Crusade events took place in Americus, Georgia, during April of 1969. It was a three-day event that featured special guests Raleigh Wynn and Dan Reeves who is part of one of my all-time favorite stories.

It took place five years earlier during the 1964 college baseball season. I loved to come back to Chapel Hill after I got out of the Air Force and watch my alma mater play. I always sat in the right field bleachers with some of my old professors like Dr. Peacock, Dr. Blythe, Coach Allen and Coach Jamerson.

UNC was playing South Carolina one day and the visiting right fielder argued a check swing call on one of the Tar Heels hitters. My loud mouth took over and I gave him a fit. After about 15 seconds of my abuse, he finally looked up at me in the stands and that made it even worse. I really let him have it then.

Back in Americus, five years later, our crusade team was being entertained in a home where three brothers were well known for their athletic abilities. Dan was playing with the Dallas Cowboys at the time and would later become head coach of the Denver Broncos, the New York Giants and the Atlanta Falcons. He would also go on to win one Super Bowl ring as a player and another as an assistant coach.

I walked up to Dan and asked him if he possibly remembered being worked over by a loud month in the right field bleachers when South Carolina played at UNC. He immediately grabbed me by the arm, looked me right between the eyes, and said, "Long, there is no way possible that you are going to tell me that it was you." I told him that it most certainly was me and everyone in the room cracked up when they heard the story. Dan could not believe it and told me that it was a good thing that he did not come up in the bleachers. We all laughed again. Just another "coincidence story."

Each Teen Crusade would typically last three days. For instance, we went to Gastonia, North Carolina and held an event at Ashbrook High School where Bobby was the featured speaker. Over 1,500 people attended the last of three meetings and a combined 600 people made decisions for Christ.

Teen Crusade lasted for six wonderful years and we traveled wherever we were needed. There's no telling how many assembly programs I spoke at during that time, especially between 1967 and 1970. It was that incredible experience that really got me thinking long term about my desire to continue evangelizing the country. Even as Teen Crusade was coming to a close, I was already planning the next phase of my ministry.

The Happenings Team: (Back row, left to right) Lester Matte, Stan Swinson and Debbie Pullen; (Middle row, left to right) Donna Stephenson, Tonya Crevier, Jan Swinson Hallenborg, Ann Swinson, Mark Dickerson and Randy Atcheson; (Front row, left to right) Cliff Barrows, Billie Barrows and Albert.

Let's Have A Happening!

In 1973, Teen Crusade still had two years of solid ministry left in it. But by then, I had set my sights on branching out. During these years, I was doing a lot of speaking and traveling on my own. I was also doing really well in the life insurance business. I could go to McDonald's, get an Egg McMuffin and leave a five-dollar tip. I never was the aggressive agent who wanted to make a million dollars. I wanted to make what I needed to make so I could go out and speak. My potential was unlimited but I didn't take full advantage of it.

When I told my company I was leaving, they couldn't believe it. They were really upset.

Can you imagine leaving a very lucrative life insurance business lock, stock and barrel, and going out on complete faith at my age with three boys that weren't even in middle school yet? I didn't even have any renewals or persistence fees from my company.

I'm thankful that Jackie was working as a nurse, so that alleviated some of the initial financial pressure.

Back in the '70s, there was a popular phrase, "Hey man, what's happening?" I loved that, so I used it to describe our events. We'd say, "We're having a happening tonight!" It was usually four nights, Sunday through Wednesday.

Early on, we incorporated and officially became known as Happenings, Inc. By 1974, I was writing a quarterly newsletter. I can remember going to the post office every other day just praying there would be a check from the newsletter to help us financially. I was happy to see a $20, $15 or $10 check—anything that would help us get through the early stages of starting a ministry. But the Lord never let us down. He always supplied our needs, and I do mean always. That's why I love Philippians 4:19 so much:

"And my God will meet all your needs according to the riches of His glory in Christ Jesus." (NIV)

I'll never forget our first "Happening" in Benson, NC, which featured George Karl and me. George was an outstanding basketball player at UNC who Bobby Jones led to the Lord. I needed a well-known athlete to bring people out before I presented the Word to them—that is, what little of the Word I knew back then.

We started the three-day event with an outdoor meeting in a placed called the Grove. About 45 minutes into the service, people started to leave. And then more people started to walk away. These people knew something was about to happen, and they were right. Seemingly out of nowhere, the wind really started to blow. We immediately announced for everyone to go the Benson Baptist Church around the corner and finished the service there during a massive thunderstorm. That night, I encountered the most gorgeous voice I'd ever heard. Her name was Donna Stephenson and she was a student at East Carolina University. After the service that night I invited her to join the Happening team, although I had no idea what our team would look like and who it would include. Over the next 25 years, Donna only missed one of our events due to illness even though she was a successful opera singer who performed for seventeen years in New York.

The success of that first event in Benson helped solidify my desire to aggressively pursue this kind of evangelistic ministry. In three nights, over 1,000 people attended and over 100 decisions were made for Christ.

In a short period of time, we added more people to the group, most of which became a core part of the Happenings team. There was Randall Atcheson, a celebrated pianist and organist player with a double major from Juilliard; Mark Dickerson, a singer and former quarterback at Mars Hill College (where a few years later we had one of the best Happenings ever on the campus there); Lester Matte, who was a fourth degree black belt in Tae Kwon Do Oh Do Kwan (who always did a fantastic job during youth night which was always packed out with young people.); Debbie Pullen, a talented young lady who performed illustrative dramas and humorous skits and was Miss Congeniality in the 1973 Miss North Carolina pageant; Dexter "Loveboat" Williams, a spectacular juggling specialist; Jesse Timmons, an Army Sergeant from Fort Bragg who testified about how God delivered him from drug addiction; Mike O'Koren, who was an All-American at UNC and NBA player; David and Mike Alexander, who were world champion cloggers that knew how to lift up the Lord through clogging; a Southern Gospel trio called The Swinsons that were as good as any trio I've ever heard; and Wes Chesson, an Atlanta Falcons wide receiver who joined us during the NFL offseason. It didn't take long for us to feel the impact Happenings ministry was having around the country. Not only were we seeing numerous decisions made at each event, letters from attendees and articles in local papers were also cropping up at a rapid pace. In early 1974, we put on a Happenings event in Lancaster, SC. Not long after that, I was sent an article that was a written by a high school student that attended for his school newspaper. It was always a special occasion for me each time these articles or letters arrived, but this one was as good as any of the hundreds of letters I received from high school students. It was called "The Letter Sweater Kid."

This guy was really different. He came on strong right at the very beginning. You felt like you were going to like him when he said his first few words. There was something about him that immediately got your attention. Was it because he was loud? Was it his enthusiasm? Was it the smile that he had on his face? No . . . I think it was because at the very beginning you knew that he was honest and believed in what he came to speak to us about. He did not "preach" to us and he did not "lecture" to us. He said that we had taught him long ago not to do that. But you knew without the preaching and the lecture exactly how he felt about, as he said it, the Master Coach. He made me think about how blessed I was when he quoted the poem about "Oh God, forgive me when I whine, because I'm blessed indeed, the world is mine." Then his illustration about the 19 year old that he saw go through "cold turkey" had to make all of us think. I certainly agreed with him when he said the one thing that turned him off concerning adults was when they said, "don't do as I do, but do as I say." He told us that the one thing we tell him that we do not like about adults today is that there are too many phonies and hypocrites. But after he agreed with that statement, he said that was the same thing he did not like about so many of us. See what I mean? He was honest, and I am certain that the large majority of us agreed with him because I don't think the students here have ever given any speaker a standing ovation like they did Albert Long . . . the "letter sweater" kid. Mr. Long, thank you for coming to be with us, and one last thing if you ever get a copy of this article. Please don't ever stop taking up for us because I think you are right . . . we are not nearly as bad as some adults think we are.

From October 24th to November 10th of that same year, I had an especially busy stretch where I was on the road 17 of 18 days and spoke 27 times in eight places in four different states. That included 19 high school assembly programs.

But the following January, something took place on the Mars Hill College Campus that I will never forget. There was no way that a Happening could have taken place except for prayer. Those college kids prepared for our event two months in advance. And then five days before we arrived, they held around-the-clock prayer in 15-minute intervals. The 96 young people that participated paved the way for an amazing three-day event. There were 1,600 students on campus and 1,200 attended every night. This is also where I met Mark Dickerson for the first time who would later became a team member. I was so pleased to get this letter from campus chaplain Robert A. Melvin:

Dear Albert:

Our entire college community has been immeasurably enriched by "Happening '75." We are deeply grateful to you and to your team for leading us in a time of genuine spiritual renewal at Mars Hill College. The rapport you established immediately with our students, the joy which was such a prominent feature of each service, and the clear appeal for Christian discipleship made these three days very important days for many individuals and, I believe, for our school.

The sheer numbers of students who attended "Happening '75" was itself a miracle. It has been several years since our entire campus shared any comparable experience. To me, the increased sense of community and the openness evident between students are among the most important contributions of the week.

One student said to me after the last service: "I can't believe the 'Happening' has lasted only three days; there have been so many experiences and changes that it would seem it would take at least three weeks for all this to happen!" In the Coffeehouse after a service, two black and two white students said they would not have believed they would be sitting together, talking like brothers, and talking about Jesus in their lives.

Bible study groups and share groups continue to meet as part of the follow-up. We pledge our best efforts to assure the continuing of the spiritual renewal begun during "Happening '75."

Sincerely yours,

Robert A. Melvin
Chaplain

The next month, February of 1975, I spoke at A.C. Reynolds High School in Asheville, NC. After the assembly, a girl came up and asked me if I remembered being there four years ago for an FCA meeting and giving a cross to a boy who was lucky to be alive from an automobile accident. I told her that I did remember everything about it, and that I also gave him a poem that went with the cross. She then told me that this boy was in full time mission work now and still had the cross with him every day.

Bill Smith, a dear friend in Charleston, West Virginia, made it possible for me to give away hundreds of those crosses with the poem "The Cross In My Pocket" by Verna Thomas. These four powerful stanzas say it all:

> *I carry a cross in my pocket*
> *A simple reminder to me*
> *Of the fact that I am a Christian*
> *No matter where I may be*

> *When I put my hand in my pocket*
> *To bring out a coin or key*
> *The cross is there to remind me*
> *Of the price He paid for me.*

> *It reminds me too, to be thankful*
> *For my blessings day by day*
> *And to strive to serve Him better*
> *In all that I do and say.*

> *So, I carry an cross in my pocket*
> *Reminding no one but me*
> *That Jesus Christ is Lord of my life*
> *If only I'll let Him be.*

I am so thankful that I have every quarterly newsletter that I wrote from 1974 until the present time. Without those newsletters this book could have never happened. I just praise the Lord for making certain that I kept them–just another "coincidence!" Here are two reports from newsletters that stood out as I was doing research:

I knew this was going to take a lot of work, and it did, but I pulled out my calendars for the past two years in order to record what my schedule consisted of, and here is what I came up with. From October 1974 through October 1976 our team had twenty "Happenings," which run from Sunday through Wednesday nights, in six different states. I spoke at seventy two high school, or middle school, assembly programs, was on fourteen different college campuses, filled pulpits fifty five times, which does not include Happening events, spoke at eighteen high school sport banquets, eight motivational banquets, twenty one civic club meetings or ladies night banquets, four pre-game, or pre-race, chapels, twelve FCA meetings or banquets, was on eight TV shows "here and there," spoke at twenty church banquets, four church conventions, had nine graduations, four baccalaureates, two PTA's, and four Christian Women Club meetings. I have no idea in the world the number of people all those engagements total, but just the high school assembly programs alone meant speaking to well over 50,000 teenagers. I have never charged a fee for a high school assembly, filling the pulpit for a church service, FCA meetings or banquets, graduations, other kinds of banquets etc. I just tell all the people who invite me, to take care of my expenses, and maybe a love offering or a donation, to go along with expenses for the ministry of Happenings, Inc. Some have been very good and many just so-so. I never accept a check made out to me and don't intend to because of a covenant I

have with my Creator. Any checks made out to me always go
to Happenings, Inc.

The other report was a combination of the first two quarters of 1984. During that six-month period, I spoke 86 times in five different states. When I discovered this, it absolutely blew my mind. Those days included, among other things, twenty-seven high school assembly programs, two four-night Happenings, three days at West Virginia State Baptist Convention, one baccalaureate and two high school graduations.

From September 8th to October 31st of that same year, I was on the road forty of those 54 days, and from November 4th to December 20th, I was on the road eleven of sixteen days. It was exhausting just making those reports for my newsletter readers and supporters. I am still exhausted after reading that.

God was so good to me, and I cannot believe that I never missed but one speaking engagement during those 25 years with the ministry because of sickness. I can remember more than once when I had to whisper through a few high school assembly programs because of laryngitis. I always had the assistance of an excellent sound system, but to help matters, I made sure to let the students know that I was going to dismiss them to study hall if they didn't pay attention. It worked every time!

As I went over those reports, I couldn't help but wonder how many total events I spoke at in thirty-five years and how many people made decisions for Christ. I can't even imagine. I'm so thankful that the good Lord kept me healthy throughout all of those years and blessed me with a wonderful wife who kept the home fires burning as much as I was gone.

Coincidental Friendships

But there's one other thing I truly cherish from those days of ministry. I met so many incredible people and forged so many long-lasting and meaningful friendships. Many of them are chronicled in the next section of this book, but there are a few of those folks that I'd like to tell you about here and the "coincidences" that put them in my life:

In 1965, Wayne Atcheson, who was the sports information director at Alabama at that time, contacted me with something like this:

> *"Albert, we have a quarterback here at Alabama that really loves the Lord and is going to a great one. He loves the poem 'I Met The Master Face To Face,' and knowing how you love poetry, I wonder if you can find it and send it to me?"*

I sent Wayne the poem and two summers later at a FCA conference at Black Mountain I met this young man who later had a brief NFL career with the Atlanta Falcons before getting into college coaching. Who would have ever thought that thirteen years later this same person would invite me to come to Lubbock, Texas to speak to his football team there at Texas Tech?

A few years later, he invited me to do the same while he was the head coach at Ole Miss. He eventually ended up working as an Athletic Director at Alabama, North Texas, UCF and Tennessee-Chattanooga, but I will best remember him for being a leader that always put God first. His name was Steve Sloan.

****

Another person I met at Black Mountain was someone who was at that time considered "The World's Strongest Man." Paul Anderson was a real favorite with the guys at all the FCA national conferences, especially when he lifted about a dozen guys up in the air while they were sitting on a table together. It was an amazing feat.

Paul won gold at the 1955 World Championships and the 1956 Olympics. He was also a two-time U.S. National Champion.

I had the pleasure of working with Paul on a couple of occasions. One of those was at Appalachian State University with Bill Wade, John Lotz and Ray Hildebrand. We were outside on campus and those students were hanging from the rafters.

I remember another occasion when I saw him in the airport in Atlanta. He was at the car rental booth and I slipped up behind him and said, "Freeze fellow. I want all your money." He never even stopped what he was doing to see what was going on. He finally turned around very slowly, looked at me, and said, "I knew it had to be someone like you Long." It was such a joy to have Paul Anderson as a friend and to have him serve on the Advisory Board of Happenings, Inc. Even though Paul was known as the strongest man in the world, I can assure you that he was much stronger for his great Lord and loved telling people all about that.

****

Dean Smith has been a good friend of mine since the early '60s, even though our beliefs concerning Christianity are as a different as night and day. In 1961, Dean took over for Frank McGuire as UNC's head basketball coach. Like so many others, he was at the FCA conference at Henderson Harbor in 1963 and a few other conferences later on at Black Mountain.

On many occasions, Dean asked Jackie and me to entertain parents years ago when that was still allowed by the NCAA. I can assure you that Dean never did anything that was illegal. That's the type of person he has always been. Dean, of course, went on to become one of the greatest NCAA basketball coaches of all time with two national championships, four National Coach of the Year honors and inductions into both the Basketball Hall of Fame and the National Collegiate Basketball Hall of Fame.

There's a picture of Dean on my wall that I treasure to this day.

On it, he wrote, "Albert, you have been a good friend for forty plus years for which I am grateful. Take good care of Jackie!"

It just breaks my heart to see him in his current physical condition. The real tragedy is that there is not yet a cure for this dreadful Alzheimer's disease. Oh Lord, make it happen!

****

Homer Rice was another very special person in my life and is still at the top of my list. I got to know him well when he became the athletic director at UNC in 1969. I was so pleased when he accepted the invitation to serve on the Board of Happenings, Inc., during the years he was in Chapel Hill.

When our son Mike accepted the job as principal of Fellowship Christian School in Roswell, Georgia in 2011, and Homer found out that Jackie and I were coming down to see their home for the first time, he immediately took over. He went out of his way to get his family together and take all of us to the country club in Atlanta for dinner. We spent three hours together and it could have easily been three more. Even though Numbers 12:3 was written about Moses, I can't think of anyone who was more humble than Homer Rice, even though Mike Kolen and Bobby Jones are right up there with him.

****

In 1971, I met another special friend at an FCA conference at Mars Hill, NC. His name was Dr. John Ed Mathison and he was the morning platform speaker. I never imagined back then that nine years later he would invite the entire Happenings team to Frazer United Methodist Church in Montgomery, Alabama for a four-night event.

During those meetings, two of John Ed's elders invited him and his wife and Jackie and me to travel with them on a tour of Jerusalem. I was absolutely spellbound by that invitation. It turned out to be a trip that we will cherish forever. I still love to tell people that "John the Methodist" baptized me in the Jordan River.

In addition to John Ed's pastoral work in Montgomery, he established John Ed Mathison Leadership Ministries with the purpose of training pastors and lay persons to impact the world for Jesus Christ and the Kingdom of God, and wrote seven books on topics such as church growth and spiritual development.

It's amazing to think that 27 years after our Happenings team ministered at his church, John Ed invited me to be a speaker at his retirement party along with Alabama governor Bob Riley and several other dignitaries. I know that I have learned much and have been greatly enriched because of my friendship with Dr. John Ed Mathison. Thank you Lord for that incredible friendship.

****

Sam Rutigliano's name is difficult to pronounce, but he is very easy to love. I first met Sam and his friend with an even more difficult name, Zenon Andrusyshyn (or "Z" as we called him), at the 1977 Appalachian State FCA conference in Boone, NC. At that time, Sam was the wide receivers coach for the New Orleans Saints and had previously been an assistant for the Denver Broncos, the New England Patriots and the New York Jets.

In the fall of 1979, Sam invited me to speak to the Cleveland Browns for their chapel service. He was in his second year as the team's head coach. I'll never forget one special thing that happened. All-Pro defensive end Lyle Alzado had just been traded to the Browns. I saw him purchasing a paper in the hotel lobby and introduced myself to him. I invited Lyle to come to chapel and explained to him that I wasn't the kind of preacher that told people they were going to hell if they didn't shape up. Not only did he show up, after the Browns won that game, he asked Sam if he could offer the prayer. In 1992, Lyle died from brain cancer that he believed was caused by his rampant steroid use, but praise God, he accepted Christ during his ordeal. That's one thing I loved about Sam. He always did his best to influence his players for Jesus. While the head coach at Cleveland, he also founded an anonymous support group known as "Coach Sam's Inner Circle," which was attended by about a dozen players. Assisted by Calvin Hill and Paul Warfield in the effort, Sam considered this group to be his greatest accomplishment as an NFL coach.

On November 14, 2007, Sam was given the National Council on Alcoholism and Drug Dependency's Bronze Key Award. A few years after his last season with the Browns, John Lotz arranged for Sam to speak at FCA one year at UNC, and in 2011, Sam was kind enough to bless our Thursday adult men's Bible study with a presentation we will never forget.

After six seasons with Cleveland, he became the head coach at Liberty University, and later the athletic director. Sam most certainly helped get our grandson Garrett to Liberty University in 2011 where he plays football. I am still blessed to have Sam as one of my dearest friends.

****

It was the fall of 1978 when I was invited to speak at a chapel service for the San Francisco 49ers before the team's game in Atlanta. When I got to the hotel, there had been a mix-up and there was no room reserved for me. That's when I ran into Les Steckel. He was a young assistant coach with the 49ers and someone I had met a few years earlier through FCA. Les was kind enough to share his room with me.

I already had great respect for him due to his service with the Marines during the Vietnam War. From San Francisco, however,

Les would go on to work for New England, Denver, Buffalo, Tampa Bay and Tennessee, where he coached in the Super Bowl. He was also an assistant at Minnesota and the team's head coach in 1984. But Les has made perhaps his biggest mark since he was named FCA's President back in 2005. He has been a great visionary for the world's largest sports ministry and helped that fine organization to continue to reach new heights. I'm still amazed when I think back to how Les took me under his wings that weekend in Atlanta.

It was just a coincidence that the good Lord allowed me to become friends with these great men of God and so many others, such as Sam, that you'll hear about in the next section of this book. But even with all these unique opportunities, the next phase of my ministry took a turn that I could have never foreseen.

The Heavy Metal Seminar

In 1984, I was at an event in Newport, Tennessee. There was bluegrass music playing and I spoke from a flatbed truck. When it was over, a man came up to me and said, "What do you know about all this rock music?"

I replied, "I don't know anything about it."

"Well didn't you say you had three boys?" he responded. "If you have three boys and you're supposed to be a motivational youth speaker, I suggest that you discover what's going on."

I really didn't know a thing about hard rock music or heavy metal. If you had asked me what KISS was, I would have said, "Something you give your wife before you go to bed at night."

When I got home, I went to the drugstore one day and was amazed at how many magazines were promoting these atrocious bands on their covers. As I did more research, I realized there was a story that needed to be told. So I got every magazine I could and learned about KISS, Black Sabbath, AC/DC, Blue Oyster Cult,

Twister Sister, Poison, Def Leppard and many more.

After reading everything I could get my hands on concerning this music and speaking at many seminars with a presentation I had worked very hard to prepare, my next step was to make an audio-cassette that allowed me to present my findings to parents, youth ministers and teens. That's when things started to go crazy. Radio stations started to call me for interviews and churches started to invite me to talk to their youth about the dangers of listening to this music.

One of my earliest and most prominent endorsements came from my dear friend of many years Barry St. Clair, director of Reach Out Ministries, who in a letter from February 12, 1985, wrote these kind words:

The heavy metal cassette came in the mail the other day. I've listened to it and was absolutely spellbound by it. You did a superb, superb job!

You're doing some great work there Albert, definitely on the cutting edge.

I know it's hard to keep up because that stuff seems like it changes every three weeks. I appreciate you staying on top of that and really relating to kids where they are in terms of that subject. I know God is going to use it to turn kids away from that kind of music and even more importantly toward the Lord Jesus.

Later that spring, the Greensboro News & Record was among several newspapers to cover one of my hard rock seminars. In that article, I had mentioned to them how, in the past year, six teenagers had committed suicide within a 22-mile radius of my home in Durham. I had researched three of those deaths and all three young people were deeply into heavy metal music or what I referred to as "a very dangerous drug."

A few years later, as these events became more popular, I took the next logical step and produced a video called "A Long Look At Hard Rock Music." Not only did I make this video available for churches and parents to purchase, I also showed large portions of it as the centerpiece of my presentations.

Up until that time, I had never realized that my sons were listening to many of the same groups I was speaking out against. So often I would holler upstairs, "If you don't turn that music down, I'm gonna come up there and throw that record player out the window!"

I even discovered my oldest son Kirk had attended every KISS concert in North Carolina that he could get to. As I began studying the personalities and music of KISS and other groups like them, I found that many of the songs were nihilistic. In other words, the lyrics conveyed the message that life is useless so live it because tomorrow you may die. Not only did the lyrics disturb me, I also started to understand that kids were subconsciously absorbing them even when they protested they'd bought the music just for the beat.

About a year into my work on the subject, my youngest son Danny came up to me one day and said, "Dad, I've never seen you work so hard on anything and I appreciate what you're doing. But I want you to know I listen to some hard rock music and I've never bought an album for the lyrics. I just enjoyed the beat."

"Do you have a favorite song right now?" I asked him.

"Yes sir."

"How many verses does it have?" I persisted.

"Three or four," he replied.

"But you don't listen to the words," I added.

"I promise you dad, I don't."

"Then quote me the first verse if you can," I said.

Danny proceeded to give me every word in all three verses–

and he'd only bought the album for the beat! It was like the Lord opened his eyes. Later on when people would say to me, "Hey, this music doesn't bother me," I responded, "How do you know it doesn't? Let me talk to your friends, to your parents and teachers and pastor. Then I'll tell you if it's affecting you."

It reminds me of the scripture in 2 Corinthians 4:4 where the Apostle Paul writes, "The god of this age has blinded the minds of unbelievers, so that they cannot see the light of the gospel of the glory of Christ, who is the image of God." (NIV)

During that time, and still today, I believe that Satan also blinds the minds of believers. Paul warns against this in Colossians 2:8: "See to it that no one takes you captive through hollow and deceptive philosophy, which depends on human tradition and the elemental spiritual forces of this world rather than on Christ." (NIV)

The music kids listen to and the videos they watch are much more than entertainment—they carry a philosophy. I always said this at my seminars: "Check out the philosophy. Scrutinize the lyrics to see what the song's really talking about, what it's teaching.' You'll often find they promote Satanism, sex, suicide and especially nihilism, which means, 'a viewpoint that traditional values and beliefs are unfounded and that existence is senseless and useless." This is exactly what that music was promoting.

Hard rock and heavy metal groups are teachers. What kind of philosophy are they teaching? What kind of values? After my presentation, someone would always comes up and say, "I can't believe you said so and so is a Satanist or devil worshipper."

But that wasn't what I had said. What I did say is to examine the words. Maybe the group isn't into Satanism or engaged in occult practices, but their lyrics may encourage it. And once again, what are these groups promoting?

I was so serious about understanding this music and the culture behind it that I actually found myself at a Motley Crue concert on February 3, 1990 at the Dean E. Smith Center on the UNC campus in Chapel Hill. No one was bigger than Motley Crue back then. They were selling out arenas all over the United States during their Dr. Feelgood World Tour.

I went to the concert with my youngest son Danny, who was 24 years old at the time, and my good friend Mark Maye, who was an outstanding quarterback at UNC at that time and is still a very good friend today. I was just a few weeks removed from my hip replacement surgery, so Danny helped me get around as I hobbled on my crutch. It was scary to see how much power these four men had over the 16,000 screaming fans that never sat down the entire time.

Drummer Tommy Lee, who wore little more than a g-string and suspenders, received the loudest roar from the fans when he decided to moon the audience. The young people made another loud noise when the inverted pentagram and a picture of Satan appeared on the screen during the laser show. It was louder than Tar Heels fans cheering a winning basket.

I sat there absolutely stunned as I watched those people absolutely mesmerized. Trust me when I say, if Motley Crue wanted to start a riot that night, 90% of those in the audience would have easily followed. That's how much they had their audience in the palm of their hands. So scary!

But the most telling part of our experience was standing in the lobby between the two shows and observing people coming and going for about 30 minutes. It was especially saddening to see many young fathers buying Motley Crue t-shirts for their young children.

My heavy metal presentation took me all across the country and into nine different states. People would show up that first night just to hear what I had to say. This is typically how I would open up each session:

"I know that many of you came tonight to hear what I had to say about your heroes. But let tell you a few things first. Number one, I'm going to be fair in everything I do. But number two, and most importantly, I'm here representing my Lord. I'm not going to hit you over the head or tell you that you are going to hell if you listen to this music. I'm not going to tell you to burn your records. I'm not God. But I'm going to be honest. If that bothers any of you, I'd appreciate if you just get up and leave. But if you'll tolerate me, I promise you this. You'll leave here at the end saying 'He's fair.' You might not agree, and most of you won't, but once again, you'll say that I was honest and fair. I'll wait and talk to any of you afterwards on one condition and that is you won't beat me up, because I'm not as fast as I used to be."

My approach was based on these instructions that the Apostle Paul gave to his young mentor Timothy:

Don't have anything to do with foolish and stupid arguments, because you know they produce quarrels. And the Lord's servant must not be quarrelsome but must be kind to everyone, able to teach, not resentful. Opponents must be gently instructed, in the hope that God will grant them repentance leading them to a knowledge of the truth, and that they will come to their senses and escape from the trap of the devil, who has taken them captive to do his will. – 2 Timothy 2:23-26 (NIV)

It didn't take long for it to become obvious just how much Satan didn't like what I was doing. I could tell you many stories of how I was personally attacked by him in ways that you would never believe, and I mean many stories. I'm telling you folks. Satan is still very much alive today. Trust me when I say he is still walking about like a roaring lion seeking whom he may devour (1 Peter 5:8). I was not one of his favorite people and many times he showed me why!

I got some very hateful letters and received phone calls at two in the morning. Usually there would be a party in the background and the caller would mock me for talking about backward masking–the practice of hiding messages within a song that can only be heard when played backwards.

At the same time, however, I received many encouraging letters from people who made the decision to stop listening to this destructive music. Hundreds of supporters also gave me strength with their consistent prayers. I promise you that those prayers are what got me through so many instances of trials and tribulations during this time.

While many hated my message, many more believed in what I was doing to reach young people. Al Menconi of Al Menconi Ministries in San Diego was one of those who had my back. I got most of my material from Al and I could not have made it without his help. He was a trailblazer in the war against pop culture's negative impact on teenagers and is still going full-speed ahead in educating our young people by helping parents communicate values to their children.

Perhaps just as important was making sure parents and youth ministers understood that if you take a "god" away from a teenager, you'd better replace it with something good. That's why I always supported contemporary Christian music as long as you could understand the words and as long as the words lifted up Jesus Christ. I told them about alternatives to the music like Petra, Rez Band and Stryper. Yes, I caught the dickens from many pastors because of my support of Christian rock. But once again, if you take a god away from someone, you had better be able to show that person how to replace his or her god with the real thing.

This extension of the Happenings ministry continued through the early 1990s, but all the while our team was still actively traveling the country holding revivals, youth assemblies and crusades. Times were changing, however, and it was clear that things wouldn't be the same for long.

Fruits of the Ministry

In the middle of the craziness surrounding my heavy metal presentations, I was still actively traveling with the Happenings team and speaking at FCA banquets and school assemblies. On April 26, 1988, I received a letter from a student that touched my heart:

Dear Mr. Long,

I had to write you tonight to thank you for helping save my life. I know you won't understand that, but I had made up my mind that I was going to commit suicide the last day this month.

At the assembly program, you made me listen. I was exactly like the person you described. People tease me because I am fat. Nobody cares about me and nobody loves me. I hate school because nobody gives me the time of day. What purpose is there in life for me?

You said everybody has a talent and I laughed at you. Then you told your story and I realized I do have a talent. Then you said suicide was a permanent solution to a temporary problem. In fact, I remember you repeating it and that really made me think. Then you said you'd get on your knees and beg anybody not to think of anything as stupid as suicide. I know you meant that, and I thought how stupid I was.

Thanks for coming to Zachary. I'll be thinking about you the last day of this month.

I love you,

(Name withheld)

P.S. Please never stop speaking to young people like me. There are many just like me. I know!

By the early 1990s, my son Mike was following in my ministry footsteps by teaching a seminar at schools called "Project Respect:

Everybody Is NOT Doing It." This abstinence program was well received throughout the area and would open the door for much bigger ministry opportunities in the near future.

In the meantime, the Happenings team was still going strong, although churches were not holding nearly as many four night events as in year's past. One of my personal highlights took place during the fall of 1993 at Campbell University in Buies Creek, NC. The Happenings Team held a tri-county crusade there featuring UNC basketball star and future NBA star Eric Montross along with his Tar Heel teammate Travis Stephenson. Donna, Mark, Randall, Lester, Debbie and the Swinson Trio did a fantastic job, but nothing could compare to the 100 public decisions that were made for Christ.

Boxes of Joy

Over the next several years, while maintaining a modest Happenings schedule, I continued to enjoy the relationships that had been built over years of ministry experiences. One weekend I'll never forget took place in the fall of 1993 and it happened thanks to one of those relationships.

Famous southern gospel singer and songwriter Bill Gaither had just started touring with some of the southern gospel's legends, but the concept was already a huge hit across the country. The "Praise Gathering" Tour made its way to Indianapolis, Indiana and my Board member Gene Anderson was able to get tickets for himself, Bob Bryan and me, along with our wives. This wasn't an easy feat to accomplish considering that the tickets had been sold out nearly a year in advance.

While there, I absolutely fell in love with Barbara Johnson, and after meeting her it was so easy to understand how every book she wrote was a best seller. Some of her more famous titles were *Stick a Geranium in Your Hat and Be Happy* and *Splashes of Joy in the Cesspool of Life*.

I missed her afternoon session because I chose to go see my friend Carl Erskine who was also speaking. Carl was another good friend I met at Henderson Harbor in 1963 and I had kept up with him ever since. When I got back, my wife Jackie just raved about Barbara and told me what I had missed by going to listen to a baseball player.

The next day, as Barbara was leaving, I ran her down and told her how my wife would never forgive me for missing her talk. She immediately gave me two cassette tapes and her latest book as she was getting into her cab.

The following weekend, I was going to Myrtle Beach to speak and I listened to both tapes on the way there and back. I laughed and cried and laughed and cried some more. When I got home, I called the number on the tape and left a message that said, "I just got home from speaking in Myrtle Beach and what a joy it was for me to take you with me."

That next Sunday, as we were having our weekly family dinner, Barbara called me and told me how much she enjoyed my telephone message. That began a special friendship until the good Lord called her home in 2007.

One of my favorite stories concerning Barbara happened two years after we first met. She called and asked me if Happenings could find a use for some of her Joy Boxes. Word Inc., had an over-abundance of these special packages, and had called her asking what she wanted them to do with the extras. I was absolutely flattered that she would even think of me.

The folks at Word told her that they would send me a skid. I had no idea what a skid was but she seemed to think that it would be maybe a hundred boxes. About ten days later, a big tractor-trailer arrived with twenty-five skids, which each contained thirty-six 12x18 boxes. There were seven Joy Boxes in each box that had to be assembled. This turned out to be 6,300 Joy Boxes!

I thought Jackie was going to collapse when she saw that tractor-trailer rolling up to our house. Thankfully a good friend from my former church allowed me to store them free of charge in his warehouse until we could figure out what to do with all of those boxes. Amazingly, it didn't take but a month before the Lord showed me how to get rid of all of them. Trust me when I say that there were so many incredible stories surrounding those Joy Boxes including how I arranged for many churches to give a Joy Box to all of their ladies on Mother's Day. I had people come from all over the state to pick up some of Barbara's Joy Boxes. She was so popular all over the country.

We had more fun laughing about that incident on numerous occasions. Yes, Jackie fully recovered after she learned that all of those boxes were going to a warehouse. But I really thought she was going to kill me when that tractor-trailer pulled up to our driveway! Just another "coincidence" how I met Barb.

Passing the Torch

By late 1997, I made the decision to have our son Mike assume the role of president at Happenings, Inc. He had been doing a lot of great work with the public schools and he had turned his "Everyone is NOT Doing It" concept into a successful four-part video series. I was very clear, however, that I wasn't retiring from ministry, just from the day-to-day operations at Happenings, Inc.

I realized the year before that four-night evangelical meetings in churches and communities were slowly but surely fading away except for the little churches that I described as "in the wildwood." It broke my heart to come to the conclusion that the talented group that we had assembled for twenty-five years to lift up our Lord was about to come to an end.

Here is a portion of what I wrote to my supporters in February of 1998:

"This will not be a farewell message to you just because Mike has taken over for his dad. As I mentioned to you in my last newsletter, I am not going to retire or even think about slowing down as long as the telephone continues to ring and He needs me for His services through the ministry of Happenings, Inc. In 1963 I accepted Jesus Christ as my Lord when I thoroughly understood what "to be born again" actually meant. It meant to resign all rights to myself…my time, my talents, my future, my all, and that was where the difficulty was…resigning myself. It meant surrendering my rights to my reputation, to my possessions, to privacy and immunity from the needs of others, and not to choose my place of service. Twenty-five years of service to Him through this ministry finally helped me to realize that. Now it is time to begin a new journey through this little ministry that I know has stood so very tall in the eyes of our great Lord these many years. We are just changing from a team that was blessed to travel all over this great land to a one-man team with Mike taking over."

A year later, although I was no longer holding Happenings meetings like before, I was able to report through the quarterly newsletters how busy the Lord was keeping me going for His glory with many speaking engagements.

Bittersweet Days

In the early 2000s, I was staying busy, but my attention was divided when my best friend John Lotz got sick with brain cancer. It was initially misdiagnosed and because of that, his fight with that dreaded disease was short. When John's wife Vicki needed to place him in a local assisted living facility, she couldn't find one that had an opening. So she called me asking for help.

For some reason, the Lord put Bucky Waters' name on my heart. Bucky was the men's basketball coach at West Virginia and then Duke during the late 60s and early 70s. He later got into sports broadcasting and became well known in the Durham area as a prominent fundraiser for Duke Children's Hospital. I called Bucky and briefly told him about Vicki's dilemma. He was going into a meeting but said he would call back soon. By the time Bucky got back with me, he had already arranged for Vicki to visit a facility the next day. Just two days after that, John moved into a place that was less than a mile from my house.

It's difficult to watch someone you care so deeply about go downhill so quickly, especially when you've known that person to be so strong, both physically and spiritually. When I wasn't on the road, there wasn't a day I didn't visit John. Sometimes I would bring him over to the house to sit on our back porch and wait for our grandchildren Garrett and Caroline to come home from school. They lived right behind us at the time. John loved them like they were his own grandchildren, and they loved him like a granddad. If we went to Chapel Hill, it would be a trip to the BP service station where all of his friends from UNC would hang out.

One time, when John was really starting to struggle, Jackie and I took John and Vicki to Chapel Hill to eat at a little place on Franklin Street. As we sat down at our table, I looked out the window and saw ESPN college basketball analyst Dick Vitale walking in. I rushed over to the door and told him I was there with John who was not doing well physically.

"Where is he?" he asked.

Dick followed me over to the table and spent a few minutes talking to John. It was a special moment that really lifted John's spirits.

About three or four years after John had died, I saw Dick working a UNC game for ESPN and made sure to catch him afterwards.

"Dick, I just want to say something to you," I said. "I'm the guy that told you about John Lotz that night in the restaurant. That was the nicest thing you did to be an encouragement to him. Vicki still talks about that today."

"I loved the guy," Dick simply responded. "Loved the guy."

When John passed away on May 5, 2001, it was a bittersweet day. I had lost one of my closest friends, but he was finally healed of that painful cancer and enjoying his new life in Heaven. I was so honored to speak at his memorial service where I made this very true statement:

"If you didn't know John Lotz, you didn't like John Lotz. But once you got to know him, you couldn't help but love him."

Losing John was tough, but it helped me appreciate my wonderful relationships even more. Bucky Waters and his wife Dottie, for instance, became close friends during this time. But it wasn't until we'd known each for about 10 years that we made an amazing discovery. It was just a coincidence when we found out that our weddings were on the exact same day (September 1) and the exact same year (1956)! So ever since, we made sure to really splurge by taking our wives to Chick-Fil-A and celebrating our anniversaries together. You know I am just kidding. It was actually Wendy's!

Speaking of my wedding anniversary, I'm reminded of another good friend named Ray Hildebrand. His hit song "Hey Paula" was a number-one radio hit back in 1963. A year later, he gave up a very lucrative career to concentrate solely on writing and singing Christian songs and to start working for FCA. Ray has been a close friend since I met him at the FCA conference at Black Mountain in 1966.

In 2006, my good friend Van Eure, the owner of the Angus Barn restaurant, hosted a celebration for me and Jackie's 50th anniversary and my 75th birthday. Ray showed up as a surprise guest. Jim Branch introduced him by saying, "To begin the evening, we have a special guest with us tonight." Ray then walked in with his guitar singing his hit song. Then he walked over to Jackie and me, told me to grab her hand, and sang a special song for us that he had written to the tune of "Hey Paula."

The event took a more spiritual turn when eight people shared about Happenings that had been held in their communities. Their testimonies of highlights that took place brought back so many memories and it was so rewarding to realize how the good Lord had used our team in so many different ways during those times.

And then our youngest son Danny held everyone captive as he concluded the evening on behalf of his older two brothers with a tribute to his mom that compared her to four different women in the Bible. Tears were flowing!

Back to the Bible

Even as we reminisced that evening about Happenings, another chapter of my ministry life was slowly taking shape. It all started a little over a year earlier at Black Mountain. Danny Lotz was in charge of the coach's Bible study every afternoon. The next to last night there, the person running the camp gave all those in attendance a sheet of paper and asked them to anonymously write down what they didn't like about themselves and some things they were struggling with in their personal lives. Danny was curious what they had to say and took the responses back to his room that night.

Now, I need my sleep, but Danny can stay up all night. So I shouldn't have been surprised when he woke me up at 12 o'clock.

"Albert, Albert!"

"What do you want Danny?"

"You've got to read these things."

"I don't want to read nothin' Danny. I want to sleep. I'll read 'em tomorrow."

About an hour later, Danny woke me up again.

"Albert, Albert!"

"Come on man! I need to get some sleep!"

So finally, at about two in the morning, Danny finally got my attention.

"Albert, get out of bed. You've got to read these things right now!"

I finally got up and Danny showed me some of the forms. About 75 percent of them mentioned pornography. It was quite an eye opener and it became clear that something needed to be done.

I'll never forget what happened the next morning at breakfast. Art Baker was one of the first guys to sit down by us and Danny told him, "Albert and I are going to start a Bible study in Chapel Hill." I had no idea in the world what he was talking about at the time.

On the way home, Danny immediately wanted to put this Bible study together. I asked him what in the world he wanted me to do. Danny wanted me to get some people together for lunch one day and discuss it. I got together with John Blanchard, who was associate athletic director at UNC, and he advised me to get in touch with Doug Shackelford, one of the top faculty members of the business school. I was amazed when Doug told me, "Albert, I've been praying for something like this to happen."

I got to work and arranged for John, Doug, Bill Cobey and Moyer Smith to meet with Danny and me for lunch. All of us agreed this was something we needed to do on campus and we all agreed to really pray about it.

The next thing I did was meet with Dick Baddour who was the athletic director at the time. I think I scared him to death.

"I don't know Albert," he said.

And I replied, "Dickey, this is not for athletes. This is for adults. We need a place to meet. That's all I want from you. I'm not going to get you in any NCAA trouble."

So he allowed us to use a room in Kenan Stadium, and that's where we started in August of 2005 with seven people. We met every Thursday from 12:15 to 1:45, which we still do today some seven years later. Danny and I would take turns leading the studies and within a year, we were up to about 30 people. Then, when we hit 40, we thought the rapture was about to happen!

In 2010, the university tore down Kenan to expand it and we had to find a new location. We went to The Bible Church off campus for about six months before landing at a more permanent host site. Now, we average about 60 to 70 every Thursday. Danny usually teaches from the Old Testament and I usually teach from the New Testament. We never talk about what we're going to do ahead of time and yet it always seems well coordinated. It's amazing how the Holy Spirit works that out.

We don't give them homework and there is no study material. The guys love it. We have bonded like you would never believe and we continue to grow. We also have a picnic each spring with the ladies group led by UNC women's basketball coach Sylvia Hatchell at her home. Over a hundred people attend each year.

You would never believe in the past seven years how many of the guys have said to Danny or me, "Why haven't I heard anything like this before?" Isn't that a tragedy? And all we do is preach the Word of God.

(Left to right) Nancy Roberts, Albert, Coach Sylvia Hatchell, Danny Lotz and Anne Graham-Lotz pose for a picture at an annual spring picnic with both the Thursday adult men's Bible study group and the UNC women's Bible study group.

Unexpected Blessings

As the Bible study was growing, some exciting things were taking place in my life. On November 13, 2007, I drove 120 miles to Mt. Airy to speak at a ladies luncheon and came back the same day and prepared to attend the FCA banquet in Raleigh that night. It just so happened to be my birthday, but it was even more special than usual.

Tom Rogeberg, special assistant to the FCA president, joined us from the national support center in Kansas City. He was there to recognize my induction into FCA's Hall of Champions. FCA has played a special part in my life and was instrumental in my salvation. So you can imagine how honored I was to be added to that distinguished group with folks like Tom Landry, Bobby Bowden, Tony Dungy, Mike Kolen, Ray Hildebrand, Carl Erskine, John Lotz, Danny Lotz, Don Shinnick, Raymond Berry, Nick Hyder, Bobby Richardson, Branch Rickey and Roger Staubach, and I could go on and on. Over the next couple of years, good friends like Ed Britton and Ken Smith were also inducted into that group.

Another turn of events took place in 2009 when the federal government cut all funding for abstinence education in public schools. My son Mike had drawn 80 percent of his income from that funding. In January of 2010, he shared with our supporters his decision to earn a Masters degree in Christian education at Southeastern Theological Seminary while cutting back on his ministry activities.

By late 2011, Mike had completed his Masters and was hired to become the principal at Fellowship Christian School in Roswell, Georgia, a suburb of Atlanta. It was a surprising twist when I took over the helm of Happenings, Inc., once again.

Like I had said back in 1998, I never retired from ministry so I was more than willing and able to get back at it. And that's what I've been doing ever since. Whether it's through the Bible study at UNC, FCA meetings, banquets and fundraisers, athletic chapel services or speaking engagements at churches, small groups and senior citizen gatherings, I am always available to be used for His glory and for the expansion of His Kingdom.

There have been so many so-called "coincidences" that have led me to this point in life–too many to mention here. That's why I've put together the next section that shares some of my most memorable stories that have taught me many wonderful lessons about walking with Jesus Christ. I pray that you will be encouraged as you read them and that you will begin to see the "coincidences" that God has arranged in *your* life, while choosing to remain anonymous.

(Left to right) Senator Jesse Helms, former U.S. Congressman and Happenings board member Bill Cobey, legendary Duke football coach Wallace Wade, Dr. Lennox Baker, Asa Spaulding Jr., and Albert in 1978.

Coach Wallace Wade was most certainly a football legend who was my friend and my neighbor. That is if you consider a neighbor one who lives about two miles from you out in the country. He had a nice farm with a lot of cattle and a split rail fence that surrounded it. Whenever it was time to load the hay on a truck, or especially when some of the rails needed replaced, he would call my friend Jack Penny (another neighbor) to "report for duty." Jack would always call me to help out because he knew how much I enjoyed just being around Coach Wade.

I'll never forget one instance as long as I live. We were putting in some new rails when he said to me, as we were talking about baseball believe it or not, that there was one person he had never met that he would like to meet. I remember to this day my response. I said "Coach, you've been on the cover of Time, Life, and numerous football magazines, every football coach and celebrity know about you, and there is someone you still would like to meet? Who in the world could that possibly be?" His answer was Bobby Richardson and I almost fainted. Almost fainted because I knew immediately that was something I could easily arrange and I told him so.

I got home and called Bobby and he thought I was putting him on since I always cut up with him when we talk, and still do. He was actually "flabbergasted," quite honored, and immediately mentioned that he wanted me to arrange that the next time he was in our area speaking. A short time later the good Lord made it happen and I took him over to meet Coach Wade. It was the first time in my life….and still is….that I ever sat with two giants and kept my mouth shut for forty five minutes as they talked. I just wish to this day that we could have recorded that conversation.

When we got in my car to leave Bobby said to me that it was the first time he could ever remember where a person knew more about those Yankee teams he played on than he did, and what a privilege it was to meet Wallace Wade. Yes, it was just a coincidence that I was there on his farm that day helping replace a split rail fence.

Each summer at the Black Mountain FCA conference Dr. Graham loves it when Danny (Lotz) brings some of the NFL and college assistant coaches to come up to the home and visit. Needless to say, this is tough on Danny as the "selection committee" because everybody wants to go. I remember well the afternoon this picture was taken. As we were departing we were all "still on cloud nine" realizing that we had been sitting there with Billy Graham for about forty five minutes and as Steve Hagan said "that was closer to heaven than I have ever been." It was a day we will never forget. A visit to Dr. Billy Graham in Montreat during the FCA conference at Black Mountain in 2010: Back row (left to right) Danny Lotz, Eddie Gram, Clyde Christensen, Albert and Dean Hood; Front row (left to right) Steve Hagan, Dr. Billy Graham and Bob Saunders.

CHAPTER ONE

BAND OF BROTHERS
God Sees Your Potential

"All the days ordained for me were written in your book before one of them came to be." – Psalm 139:16b (NIV)

Everyone has the potential to do great things because God creates everyone with greatness in mind.

Let me share for a moment the story of five teenagers from Durham High School. It was 1949 when I went with Roger Craig, Jack Stallings, Harry Lloyd and Julius Moore to the local ballpark to see the Boston Red Sox play the Cincinnati Reds in an exhibition game.

During the game, I caught a foul ball and stayed after the game to get some autographs from a few players like Johnny Pesky, Bobby Doerr, Dom DiMaggio, Hank Sauer and Dave "Boo" Ferriss. Who would have ever thought that 14 years later I would meet Dave at the FCA national conference at Henderson Harbor, New York where my life was changed? And who knew that in another 14 years, Dave would invite me to speak at his church in Cleveland, Mississippi? That was quite a coincidence that the Lord put together.

But the important part of this story is what happened to the five of us that went to that baseball game back in 1949.

Roger Craig went on to play professional baseball for the Brooklyn and Los Angeles Dodgers, the St. Louis Cardinals, the Philadelphia Phillies, the Cincinnati Reds, and the New York Mets where he pitched the first game in that expansion team's history. Roger was the pitching coach for the Detroit Tigers and the Houston Astros and he managed the San Diego Padres and San Francisco Giants for a combined 10 years. He ended his career with four World Series rings, three as a player and one as a coach.

Jack Stallings became a successful college baseball coach for 39 seasons and 1,257 career wins. He spent 36 of those seasons at Georgia Southern where he led his teams to one College World Series appearance, six NCAA postseason appearances and seven conference championships. Jack also coached 22 All-Americans at Georgia Southern and his jersey was the first to be retired by that program.

Harry Lloyd turned out to be a legendary high school baseball coach. He was the head coach at The Westminster Schools in Atlanta for 37 years and led that team to three Georgia state championships. Harry also managed in the Philadelphia Phillies minor league system for three years and has since been inducted into in the Georgia Athletic Coaches Hall of Fame.

Julius Moore was the most outstanding high school pitcher in the South. He signed with the New York Yankees and was on the fast track to the big leagues. But after serving in Korea and being discharged from the Army, Julius broke his right wrist in an automobile accident not long before he was supposed to report for spring training. That injury may have ended his athletic career, but it didn't keep him from making a difference. Julius joined the police force and later fought crime as a detective in the Durham area.

A few years after my four-sport career at the University of North Carolina, I accepted the Lord as my Savior and followed Him into the ministry with Teen Crusade and later Happenings Inc., both of which made it possible for me to talk to thousands of people about the peace, love and joy of knowing Jesus Christ.

We were just an average bunch of kids back then, but God saw the potential in each of us. He took the seemingly ordinary and did some extraordinary things. And yes, it was just a coincidence that all of that happened. – *AL*

God Sees Your Potential

Eons before Albert and his four friends were born, God already knew who they would become. He had given each of them the ability to do great things and the tools to be excellent at whatever occupation they might choose.

The same is true for every single person who ever enters into this world. That doesn't mean everyone will necessarily win a World Series, become a hall of fame coach, serve the public in a lofty position, or minister to thousands of people across the country. But when it comes to how God views greatness, we are all born with the gifts and talents necessary to impact our world in some form or fashion.

The Bible gives us three specific reasons why this is true. First of all, we learn that from the very beginning of this earth's history, mankind was meant for greatness simply by virtue of the Creator Himself:

"So God created man in his own image, in the image of God he created him; male and female he created them." – Genesis 1:27

Secondly, and on a more personal level, David writes that God has lovingly handcrafted each and every one of us and has "ordained" all of our days:

"For you created my inmost being; you knit me together in my mother's womb. I praise you because I am fearfully and wonderfully made; your works are wonderful, I know that full well. My frame was not hidden from you when I was made in the secret place, when I was woven together in the depths of the earth. Your eyes saw my unformed body; all the days ordained for me were written in your book before one of them came to be." – Psalm 139:13-16

And finally, God gave us the perfect example of what greatness looks like through the example of His Son Jesus Christ. It's not about doing what is great in the eyes of men, although God does use those things for His purpose, but it's really about fulfilling the two great commandments:

"Love the Lord your God with all your heart and with all your soul and with all your mind. This is the first and greatest commandment. And the second is like it: Love your neighbor as yourself." – Matthew 22:37-39

That's what true greatness looks like in God's eyes. It might come in the form of national exploits or simple acts of kindness. Either way, we all have the potential for greatness. Now, it's simply up to us to recognize that potential, step out in faith, and fulfill His extraordinary purpose for our seemingly ordinary lives.

Life Long Lesson
God sees your potential and so should you.

Going Long

1. When you come across people in your daily life, do you see them as having great potential or simply as ordinary individuals with no great significance?

2. What are some things that might cause someone not to see their potential? Have you struggled with those things?

3. What are some things that might cause someone not to reach their full potential (even if they know it's there)? Again, have you ever found yourself in that situation?

4. What have you done so far to set your potential into motion? Where does God's will for your life fit into your desire to fulfilling your potential?

5. Make a list of things that you believe you have the potential to accomplish. Now make a list of things that have kept you from accomplishing those things.

6. Read Genesis 1:27 and Psalm 139:13-16. How do those scriptures inspire you to get the most out of your God-given gifts? What can you start doing today that will set you on the path towards fulfilling your potential?

Today's Prayer: Lord, I believe that you created me to do great things. Help me to recognize my potential. Show me what true greatness looks like and then give me the courage to step out in faith and fulfill Your purpose for my life.

CHAPTER TWO

THE FOUR-LETTER KID
God Always Has a Plan

"Before I formed you in the womb I knew you, before you were born I set you apart; I appointed you as a prophet to the nations." – Jeremiah 1:5 (NIV)

God wanted me to be a four-sport letterman at North Carolina. There's no doubt in my mind. If I hadn't competed in four sports for the Tar Heels, I might not be writing this book. Oh, I'm sure that God would have still used me even without my unique college athletics history. But looking back, it's clear that He was able to open doors for me because of it.

Before I get into how things happened at North Carolina, it might be good to explain how I got to Chapel Hill in the first place. I was a four-sport athlete at Durham High School, but all I ever wanted to do was play professional baseball. College ball was going to be my first big step towards that dream.

My success at Durham brought attention to what I was doing in other sports. I was the safety and kick returner and then the quarterback for our football team that won two state championships. We never lost a game. Both years we were invited to go down to Miami, Florida to play in the Kiwanis Bowl at the Orange Bowl against Miami Senior High School. The Kiwanis Bowl took the best team in the South against the best team in the Miami area. We went down there and whipped up on them the first year and then the second year we beat them again primarily because of Worth Lutz who was our "all everything back" on those two teams.

So when the football recruiters came around, I told them not to touch me. And nobody did. But in 1951, I did end up going to North Carolina on a half baseball, half basketball scholarship.

Now keep in mind, I had no intentions of playing anything but baseball and basketball for the Tar Heels. But everything changed during my freshman year. Around Christmas time, they decided to fire head football coach Carl Snavely and the new staff was going to replace his single-wing offense with the straight T-formation. There were six or seven single-wing tailbacks in the program, but they didn't have a quarterback. That's when they started recruiting me. They wined me and dined me and talked about what it was like to run out on the field with 40,000 people in the stands. That sounded nice and all, but what sold me was the $15 a month I would get for laundry money. Living in Durham, my momma could wash my clothes for me, and that $15 back then was like $150 today.

But then the coaches told me, "Albert, you've got to understand, you'll miss your first year of baseball. We're bringing in Otto Graham to work with the quarterbacks and you *must* make spring practice." So I agreed to do it.

While we were practicing during the spring of my freshman year, the head track coach Dale Ranson and his assistant came to talk to me. They wanted me to help them with the broad jump. Of course they call it the long jump today. I was an All-State track athlete back in high school and the coaches felt like I could score some extra points for the team. I went through the entire spring football practice and then I worked on getting my steps down for the broad jump. And I just had to hit a ball, so I was playing on the JV baseball team at the same time.

When the conference track meet came around, I did well enough to make the finals and that automatically earned me a letter for the season even though I'd already qualified for one before that event. That was the only track letter I would ever earn. I participated three years in football, three years in baseball, two years in basketball and one year in JV basketball. Most importantly, I had earned the distinction of lettering in four sports–a rare accomplishment that would stick with me for years.

I didn't even know the Lord then. I was a good boy. I didn't cuss. I went to church every other week. I didn't smoke or drink, except maybe a beer or two. I was basically a good guy. It's funny how God works. Little did I know at the time that He had arranged two "coincidences," the first that put me on the football team and the other that gave me the opportunity to earn that one letter in track.

I wouldn't understand just how important that one letter was until a little later in life, but I know now that God always had it figured out–even when I didn't have a clue what was going on. – *AL*

God Always Has A Plan

When Albert arrived on the North Carolina campus in Chapel Hill, he had a plan. In his mind, it was a pretty good plan. And for the talented young athlete from Durham, there was nothing wrong with wanting to pursue his dreams to play professional baseball. But it didn't take long for the road to fork in a direction that he never anticipated.

The opportunity to play football and then the chance to participate in track (even if for just one brief season) opened the door for Albert to accomplish something that rarely happened during that era and never happens today. It turns out, his four-sport feat was the only time it took place in ACC history and was just the second time in his school's history. About 10 years earlier (1939-41), the legendary Brooklyn Dodgers second baseman Jackie Robinson completed a similar four-sport stint at UCLA.

Albert was never a famous professional athlete like Robinson, but as you'll read later on in this book, his notoriety as a four-sport athlete played an important part in his ministry and opened the door to some significant opportunities.

The Bible tells us about another multi-talented young man named David. If there were competitions to match his long list of abilities, he might have lettered in sports like sheep herding, lion wrestling, slingshot shooting and sword fighting. David was also a gifted musician with a profound talent for singing, playing and writing inspirational songs.

As a young shepherd boy, David didn't know it, but God was grooming him to do big things. He was developing David to be a great warrior, leader and spiritual voice. It might have seemed like a coincidence that David stumbled upon the battlefield at the exact same time that the Philistine giant Goliath was mocking the Israelites. But David was simply walking out the steps that God had already mapped out for him.

David's faithfulness fueled his defeat of Goliath and the entire Philistine army. His recognition that God had a plan for his life eventually led him to the throne where he succeeded Saul as the king. And still today, we read his Book of Psalms for daily guidance and encouragement.

What David experienced as a boy is really no different than what Albert experienced as a college athlete. And if we will individually step back and look at the big picture of our own lives, we will also realize that God is working things out for our present and for our future. But too often, we don't see beyond our finite, earthly worldview. We get caught up in our daily routines, our financial struggles, our interpersonal conflicts and our selfish desires, and we end up completely overlooking the little things that happen all around us, right under our noses.

There are doors He wants us to walk through. There are closed doors He wants us to walk away from. There are people in our path that He wants us to engage. There are greater goals that He wants us to pursue. And it's all because God has a purpose and plan for our lives. He knows exactly what He's up to and His dream is to see us walking out a fulfilled, active life of faith.

In Jeremiah 1:5, God tells each of us that He knew us and set us apart even before we were even conceived in our mother's womb. And even better, He gave us a purpose—to be prophets to the nations. Later on in that same Old Testament book, God gave another incredible promise:

"For I know the plans I have for you," declares the LORD, "plans to prosper you and not to harm you, plans to give you hope and a future." – Jeremiah 29:11

That's why we must trust that no matter what our circumstances are now, God has a plan. And as Albert can certainly testify, it's a good plan and much better than anything we could map out on our own. When things start to go in a completely different direction than what we'd hoped or when disappointments start to usher fear and doubt into our hearts and minds, that's the time to celebrate the simple truth that God has it all figured out—even when we don't have a clue what's going on. – CB

Life Long Lesson
Trust that God always has a plan and He is actively working in your life to ensure that His plan is fulfilled.

Going Long

1. What are some plans that you have made for your life? Have those plans worked out? Have they fallen through? Are they still in progress?

2. Are there any parts of Albert or David's stories to which you can relate? Explain.

3. Read Jeremiah 1:5. What does that scripture mean to you personally?

4. Read Jeremiah 29:11. Does that verse resonate with you or does it challenge your faith?

5. What are some things that you can do today that will help you better trust the fact that God has a plan for your life?

Today's Prayer: Lord, help me to embrace your purpose and plan for my life. Even when I don't completely understand what that looks like or when it will come to pass, give me the patience, the strength and the faith to believe that you have my best interest in mind. I trust you Lord and eagerly await what You have in store for me!

CHAPTER THREE

THE LETTA SWEATTA
God Humbles The Proud

"For whoever exalts himself will be humbled..." - Matthew 23:12a (NIV)

Pride is a dangerous thing. Those who don't allow the Lord to root it out of their hearts will be headed for trouble.

When I was in high school, my one great source of pride was my letter sweater. I was so wrapped up in my athletic performance and that sweater became my god. When I started speaking at FCA events and sports banquets, it became the subject of my trademark story. It really resonated with those young athletes.

The story was an exaggerated version of how much I loved that sweater. In fact, I even made sure to overemphasis my North Carolina accent. I called it my "letta sweatta."

I really laid it on thick. I bragged about how that "sweatta" reached all the way from my shoulder across my great, big beautiful muscles, right down my fingertips. Those kids got a real kick out of that story, but at the same time, it spoke deep into their hearts.

In reality, I was never one who was overly boastful or prideful. I can guarantee you my dad would have never allowed that to happen. He was an elementary school principal for nearly 40 years and always kept me straight.

One night, I came home after a big basketball game at Durham High School. I had played particularly well and I couldn't sleep. I was too excited thinking about my performance on the field. I stayed up until early the next morning and waited for the morning paper. I was anxious to see my name on the printed page.

While I was reading about myself, my dad came into the room and taught me a lesson that I would never forget. He gave me a poem by Saxon White Kessinger called "The Indispensable Man." It was his gentle way of reminding me that I should never allow myself to get too big for my britches. One section of that poem was especially powerful:

Take a bucket and fill it with water,
Put your hand in it up to the wrist,
Pull it out and the hole that's remaining
Is a measure of how you'll be missed.

I'm so glad I learned that lesson at a young age. It made it easier to deal with some disappointments I experienced at the University of North Carolina. Although I was a four-sport athlete there, things didn't always go as well as I'd hoped. I left all the "fame and glory" at Durham High School and went from the big fish in the little pond to a little minnow in the big lake.

To make matters worse, the football team struggled mightily throughout my career and never won more than four games in a season. I used to poke fun of that humbling experience when talking to various groups and tell them how our team held a victory celebration if we won the coin toss before the game, and how I called for a fair catch on every hike because our offensive line was so bad.

Even though I always considered myself a Christian, I wasn't following the Lord during those years in high school, college and the first few years after I graduated. I'm thankful that my father paved the way for me to have a better understanding of how important it is to avoid getting caught up in a prideful spirit, especially over something as insignificant as a high school "letta sweatta." –
AL

God Humbles The Proud

When Albert was tempted to become prideful about his athletic accomplishments, long before he discovered who his real wise Father was, he thankfully had a wise earthly father who quickly put him on the path towards a more humble approach. He later learned in college the harsh truth that success is often short lived. It's never a good idea to place too much value on accolades and personal achievement.

Countless others haven't been so fortunate. The sports world, for instance, has presented far too many examples of individuals that took a major tumble after allowing their on-field exploits to swell them up with pride. King Solomon's wise but cautionary words bear out this reality:

"Pride goes before destruction, and haughtiness before a fall." – Proverbs 16:18 (NIV)

Hundreds of years later, Jesus preached a sermon about pride and included this parallel spiritual truth:

"For whoever exalts himself will be humbled." – Matthew 23:12a (NIV)

Still, we as fallible humans can't seem to help ourselves. Even though we've seen the negative results of prideful living, we are daily tempted to think more highly of ourselves than we should (as the Apostle Paul talks about in Romans 12:3). But thankfully, there are some steps we can take to root out this awful condition:

1. **Admit that pride is a problem**: Before we can deal with pride, we first must recognize that we were all born into this world as sinners and with pride in our hearts:

"Surely I was sinful at birth, sinful from the time my mother conceived me." - Psalm 51:5 (NIV)

2. **Ask the Holy Spirit to reveal areas of pride in your heart**: Sometimes we don't even realize how pride is negatively affecting us and we need His help to see exactly what kind of pride we are fighting against:

"Search me, O God, and know my heart; test me and know my anxious thoughts. See if there is any offensive way in me, and lead me in the way everlasting." - Psalm 139:23-24 (NIV)

3. **Allow the Holy Spirit to change you**: While pride is a condition that comes from the heart, it also impacts our thinking, and we need a supernatural intervention:

"Do not conform to the pattern of this world, but be transformed by the renewing of your mind." - Romans 2:2a (NIV)

4. **Be vigilant against pride**: The enemy is always lurking around the corner and looking for a way to tempt us with prideful attitudes. It's a daily fight that requires proactive attention:

"Submit yourselves, then, to God. Resist the devil, and he will flee from you." - James 4:7 (NIV)

5. **Follow Jesus' example**: Even though He had every reason to be prideful, the Son of God always exhibited a humble spirit:

"Your attitude should be the same as that of Christ Jesus: Who, being in very nature God, did not consider equality with God something to be grasped, but made Himself nothing, taking the very nature of

*a servant, being made in human likeness. And being found in
appearance as a man, He humbled Himself and became obedient to
death–even death on a cross!" – Philippians 2:5-8 (NIV)*

Resisting pride isn't easy, but with the Lord's help, we can avoid
some of life's unnecessary heartaches and pains. – CB

**Life Long Lesson
When you're tempted to think too highly of yourself,
remember that God humbles the proud.**

Going Long

1. What are some different manifestations of pride? Which of those
have you struggled against in your life?

2. Why do you think pride is so difficult to resist?

3. Read Proverbs 16:18 and Matthew 23:12. What are some ways
that pride can cause someone to stumble or even take a hard fall?
Can you think of a time when pride stirred up trouble in your life?

4. Go through each of the five steps in the fight against pride.
Which of these steps have you implemented in your life? Which of
these steps have been missing or inconsistently utilized? What differences do you notice in those times you are actively fighting
against pride versus those times when pride seems to have the
upper hand?

5. What are some things you can start doing today that will help
you take a stronger stand against pride in your life? How do you
think dealing with pride in a more consistent manner might make
your life better?

Today's Prayer: Lord, search my heart for any remnants of pride. Holy Spirit, convict me when I give in to pride. Correct me and set me back on the path of Christ-like humility. I want to be more like You.

CHAPTER FOUR

A POWERFUL WITNESS
God Wants To Preserve
Your Influence

"If anyone causes one of these little ones–those who believe in me–to stumble, it would be better for them to have a large millstone hung around their neck and to be drowned in the depths of the sea."
– Matthew 18:6 (NIV)

Some of the greatest lessons we learn in life take a little bit of time before they sink in. The first time we hear them, they make no sense to us. But then something happens later on that brings back what we once learned and everything just clicks.

That's what happened to me in 1963 on my first trip to an FCA conference in Henderson Harbor, NY. Traveling with my close friends Danny and John Lotz, we stayed at their parents' home in North Port the night before. The next day, we took off for the conference and what was supposed to take one hour turned into a four-hour drive.

We had plenty of time to talk and one of our conversations was about drinking beer. I loved beer as an adult–especially after a softball game. I'd come home, prop my feet up and pop a couple of beers. But on this road trip, Danny and John were arguing with me about it. They didn't think I should be drinking beer and after a while I started to get ill with them.

So I said, "Okay guys! I'm not into the Bible like you are. I don't even know how many books are in the Bible. But you show me anywhere in the Bible where it says, 'Thou shall not drink a good cold beer after a softball game' and I'll quit drinking!"

Then Danny turned to me and replied, "Albert, I can't show

you anything in the Bible that says that, but I can show you plenty of scriptures like Matthew 18:6, Mark 17:2 and Luke 9:42 where it says, 'If you cause any of these little ones to stumble, it's worse than having a millstone put around your neck and dropped into the deepest part of the ocean.'"

At the time, that meant nothing to me.

As you've already read in the first section of this book, everything changed at Henderson Harbor when I asked Christ to come into my life. Two days later, I was sitting in Shea Stadium watching my good friend Roger Craig pitch for the New York Mets. It wasn't long after I settled in when the vendor came through my section.

"Beer here! Beer here!"

I had a quarter in my pocket and that's what a beer cost back then. As I reached in to get that quarter, I said, "Lord, I still don't understand what happened to me this week, but if you let me get by with this beer right here today, it'll be the last one that ever touches my lips." When the Lord turned the water into wine, I don't think it could have compared to that beer. It was the greatest beer I ever drank in my life–and one has never touched my lips since.

Now, I'm not saying anything against anyone who has a good cold beer after a softball game or anyone who has a glass of wine with their meal. But when things get out of control, that's when you need to watch out:

"Do not get drunk on wine, which leads to debauchery. Instead, be filled with the Spirit." – Ephesians 5:18

About a month later, something happened that really opened my eyes. My wife Jackie was working as a nurse. I was at home taking care of the boys and watching the Major League Baseball "Game of the Week." I got my son Kirk out of bed and held him in my arms as I relaxed in my lazy back chair. It just so happened that the sponsor for the game was Falstaff Brewery. That was the beer that I used to drink. When the commercial came on, Kirk looked up at me and said, "Daddy, why did you stop drinking beer?" He asked me that question because, I'm embarrassed to say, I used to give him a sip or two.

All of a sudden, I remembered those scriptures that Danny Lotz quoted to me. Until that very moment, I didn't know what they meant, but now it was plain as day. Not only was God protecting my witness for the future when I'd be traveling the country as a youth evangelist, He was keeping me from being a stumbling block for my own children. As I held Kirk with tears in my eyes, the first thought that came to mind was simply, "Thank you Lord!"

Yes, everything that happened in this story was just a coincidence. – *AL*

God Wants To Preserve Your Influence

At first glance, it might seem like Albert's story is about an age-old debate within the church. Is it okay for Christians to consume alcoholic beverages or should they abstain? But it's really much bigger than that. While we as believers often want to focus on individual issues, God's Word lets us know that we really need to be more concerned about how our lifestyle choices are impacting our influence on the world.

In other words, are the things that we do in our daily lives upholding or harming our Christian witness?

For the modern day church, the question usually revolves around things like alcohol and also includes debates about tobacco, tattoos, entertainment and a wide array of social issues.

But for the early church, one of the big issues was the consumption of food that had been sacrificed to idols. Many Christians believed it was sacrilegious and sinful to partake of this tainted meat. The Apostle Paul argued that because idols are "nothing at all in the world" and because "there is no God but one," that the sacrifice itself was meaningless and did no harm to the meat (1 Corinthians 8:1-6). Paul then conceded that not everyone was spiritually strong enough to understand that truth and therefore still believed that the food was "defiled" because it had "been sacrificed to a god." (1 Corinthians 8:7)

So Paul basically makes the case that it's okay to eat meat that has been sacrificed to idols. But then he adds a warning to his teaching.

"Be careful, however, that the exercise of your rights does not become a stumbling block to the weak. For if someone with a weak conscience sees you, with all your knowledge, eating in an idol's example, won't that person be emboldened to eat what is sacrificed to idols? So this weak brother or sister, for whom Christ died, is destroyed by your knowledge. When you sin against them in this way and wound their weak conscience, you sin against Christ. Therefore, if what I eat causes my brother or sister to fall into sin, I will never eat meat again, so that I will not cause them to fall." – 1 Corinthians 8:8-13

Like Albert and his decision about drinking beer, Paul chose not to partake in something that he knew was not necessarily sinful because, at that point in history, he knew eating the sacrificed meat could cause others to be confused, and even worse, could cause others to stumble and possibly sin against God. Paul realized it was more important to preserve his significant influence rather than give in to his fleshly desires. The Apostle explains it this way:

"'I have the right to do anything,'" you say–but not everything is beneficial. 'I have the right to do anything'–but I will not be mastered by anything. – 1 Corinthians 6:12

And in his letter to Timothy, Paul gives some good advice that was originally aimed at young people, but that should be heeded by Christians of all ages:

"Set an example for the believers in speech, in conduct, in love, in faith and in purity." – 1 Timothy 4:12b

Albert discovered when he made the decision to stop drinking beer that it wasn't just about causing young Christians to stumble or being a good example for his children. Setting aside things that might send a wrong message became vitally important when he entered the ministry and began traveling the country and sharing the Gospel with teenagers and young adults.

That's not to say that we will never make mistakes or make poor choices once we accept Christ. There is no one perfect but Him and we can only do our best–with the Word of God and His Spirit as our guide–to live upright and blameless before the world. And as we walk out our relationship with the Lord before others, He will use our witness as a means by which we can influence those closest to us, and even those who might be watching from a distance.

In light of God's call to each of us, we must make some hard choices about how we are going to exercise our freedom as His children. Will we allow the world to influence us and diminish our witness, or like Albert, will *we* be the influencers and allow God's light to shine through us and lead others back to Him? – *CB*

Life Long Lesson
God wants to preserve your influence so that
He can be glorified in your life.

Going Long

1. Read 1 Corinthians 6:12. What do you think Paul meant when he said, "not everything is beneficial" and "I will not be mastered by anything"?

2. What is an example of something in today's society that might not necessarily be a sin against God but that could become a stumbling block for others?

3. Read 1 Timothy 4:12. Go through each of those things mentioned (speech, conduct, love, faith and purity) and discuss how becoming lax in those areas might negatively impact a Christian's witness?

4. How is a Christian's witness directly related to influence? Give some examples of how a Christian's witness can increase his or her influence. What are some examples of how a Christian's witness can decrease his or her influence.

5. What are some things that you can start doing today that will strengthen your Christian witness and allow you to have greater influence on others for the sake of the Gospel?

Today's Prayer: Lord, search my heart and reveal to me things that are diminishing my witness as a child of God. Help me root out any unnecessary things that are not beneficial–things that might cause one of Your children to stumble or decrease my influence on this world. As Paul wrote in Romans 12:1, I want to be a living sacrifice so that others will be drawn to You.

CHAPTER FIVE

UNASHAMED CHRISTIAN
God Empowers The Bold

"For I am not ashamed of the gospel, because it is the power of God that brings salvation to everyone who believes: first to the Jew, then to the Gentile." – Romans 1:16 (NIV)

Someone missed a shot, but it sure wasn't me. Even though my playing days at North Carolina where behind me, I was still as competitive as ever. That was certainly the case in 1958 when I took to the court with some of my fellow Shaw Air Force Base football players against the Bobby Richardson All Stars in a charity game at Sumter, South Carolina, benefitting the March of Dimes.

I knew all about Bobby's early career with the New York Yankees. He had just finished his fourth year with the club and was one of Major League Baseball's rising stars. So when his team got the rebound, Bobby was running down the court looking for the open pass. I thought to myself, "He's gonna' be moving, but I'm gonna' draw that foul!"

When he caught the ball, I was waiting for him. Bobby was already running at full speed so when he turned and saw me, in one quick motion, dribbled the ball right between my legs, caught up with it and went in untouched for a layup. I was humiliated.

A few years later, we became close friends and this is how he tells that story:

"I didn't know Albert back then, but I knew that I'd better not go up for a layup the rest of the night if he was guarding me because I would've been up in the first row of the bleachers."

I always like to correct him by saying, "He's wrong! He would've been up in the *third* row of the bleachers!"

Before I met Bobby, I had one of his baseball cards. The Bible verse Romans 1:16 was printed on the back. But back then, that scripture meant absolutely nothing to me. It sure does mean something to me now. That's because Bobby lived that verse every day and showed me what it looked like to be a bold, unashamed witness for Christ.

In one interview, Bobby was asked if being a Christian helped make him a better second baseman. Without even thinking, here's how he replied:

"Absolutely. Being a Christian helps me be a better husband. It helps me be a better father. It helps me be a better person. So if being a Christian helps me be a better husband, a better father and a better person, then certainly it helps me be a better second baseman. It doesn't mean the Lord is going to let me get the winning base hit every time. He's not handling that part of it. But it sure does help me."

Bobby wasn't just any second baseman. After 11 years with the Yankees, he had played in eight All-Star Games and had won five gold gloves. Bobby played in seven World Series and was a key part of three championship teams. In 1960, he became the one and only member of a losing team to be named World Series MVP. And in 2000, the *New York Daily News* named Bobby the starting second baseman for the all-time Greatest Yankees Team.

But Bobby didn't let his fame change him. He was never ashamed to talk about the Lord. And Bobby never compromised his Christian faith. That's why 11 years after that basketball game, I wasn't surprised to hear from him and Sam Anderson, the pastor of a small Presbyterian church in Kershaw, SC. The two had decided to start a ministry called Teen Crusade. They asked me to do the high school and middle school assemblies and be the emcee for the nightly meetings.

Teen Crusade ministry lasted for five wonderful years and we traveled anywhere people wanted us. That was when my friendship with Bobby really blossomed. Several years later, his bold witness helped lead his Hall of Fame teammate Mickey Mantle to a relationship with Jesus Christ. When Mickey passed away in 1995, Bobby spoke at the funeral and made sure to share the Gospel with the thousands of people in attendance.

To this day, I consider Bobby to be one of my closest friends in the world. It was just a coincidence that our relationship actually began when he dribbled the ball between my legs that night. – *AL*

God Empowers The Bold

Through Bobby Richardson's example, Albert was able to see a picture of Godly boldness. Bobby had every reason *not* to share his faith publicly. At the height of his career, he risked ridicule and alienation in exchange for righteousness and a fulfilling relationship with the Lord.

In the New Testament, we read about one of the boldest men of God to walk the earth. His name was Paul and he was responsible for a large portion of the Bible's seminal teachings. It wasn't popular to be a follower of Christ during that time. In fact, identifying yourself as a Christian was often a dangerous proposition resulting in imprisonment, torture and death. Yet despite the cost, Paul wrote these powerful words to the early Church.

> *"For I am not ashamed of the gospel, because it is the power of God that brings salvation to everyone who believes: first to the Jew, then to the Gentile." – Romans 1:16 (NIV)*

There are three keys that will allow us to get to the point where we too can speak those words and, more importantly, live them out.

1. Confidence in Christ – If we truly believe that Jesus is the Son of God and we truly believe that He is living in our hearts, we will have the confidence to ask God for the strength to do what He has asked us to do. Paul reiterates this point in his letter to the Church at Ephesus:

"In him and through faith in him we may approach God with freedom and confidence." – Ephesians 3:12 (NIV)

2. Confidence in our Purpose – Once we understand our true purpose in life–to glorify God and share the message of hope with others–we will be empowered to walk out our calling and suppress any fear that might be keeping us from accomplishing that mission. Paul models this truth in a prayer request presented to the early Church:

"...And (pray) also for me, that words may be given to me in opening my mouth boldly to proclaim the mystery of the gospel." – Ephesians 6:19 (ESV)

3. Confidence in our Walk – We cannot earn our salvation. That can only come through the power of Jesus' blood. But as we strive to live like Him, we can be confident in knowing that walking upright before God and men will preserve our witness and empower us to be unashamed in our presentation of the Gospel. This is how King Solomon explains that truth:

"The wicked flee though no one pursues, but the righteous are as bold as a lion." – Proverbs 28:1 (NIV)

Being bold takes a sizeable step of faith, but once we understand from whence our confidence originates, like Albert's good friend Bobby Richardson, the Apostle Paul and so many other great men and women of faith, we too can be unashamed witnesses to the power and glory of God's great love. – *CB*

> **Life Long Lesson**
> **God empowers the bold**
> **through a confidence in His Son Jesus Christ.**

Going Long

1. What are some reasons why it might be difficult for a famous athlete like Bobby Richardson to be bold about his faith? What about Paul? How do you think his circumstance potentially made a bold faith problematic?

2. What are some common circumstances or emotions that might cause someone to lack boldness in their walk with the Lord?

3. What are some things that have hindered you from being a bold, unashamed witness for Christ?

4. Go back and read the three keys to confidence and their adjacent scriptures. Which of these three areas are most challenging for you and why? How do you think those verses might help you build up more confidence as a follower of Christ?

5. What are some things that you can start doing today that will help increase your confidence in Christ and begin to live out a more bold faith?

Today's Prayer: Lord, give me more confidence in You and in my purpose. Give me the strength to walk upright before the world. Through all of these things, make me a bold, witness of Your power and glory in my life. I want to walk unashamed of the Gospel so that I might reach others for You!

Albert kneels with a portrait depicting him during his football playing days at the University of North Carolina.

Albert during his football
playing days at UNC.

(Left to right) Dr. Fred Schoonmaker,
Albert, Charlie Scott, John Lotz and
Dave Chadwick at
Black Mountain in 1967.

(Left to right) Coach Hennen, Ben Carnevale, Dean Smith and Bob Davies listening
to Coach Johnny Orr at the FCA conference at Henderson Harbor, NY in 1963.

(Left to right) Maxie Baughan, James Jeffrey, Bill Wade, Carroll Dale and Ron Morris at Black Mountain in 1967.

(Left to right) Billy Zeoli, Clebe McClary, Albert and Bobby Richardson talk strategy at a pick-up basketball game during one of the group's Teen Crusade functions.

Raymond Berry (seated) and (standing left to right) Albert, Calvin Thielman and Bobby Richardson with Katherine Bryson in her iron lung at Black Mountain in 1968.

Former UNC basketball star Mike O'Koren during a Happening in Asheville, NC with Granny Schreiber, Albert's good friend Jim Schreiber's mother.

(Left to right) Coach Sam Rutigliano, Zenon "Z" Andrusyshyn and Albert at the FCA conference at Appalachian State University in Boone, NC.

Albert (middle) with Ned Jarrett (left) and Dale Jarrett (right) at a Happening in Conover, NC.

Albert (far right) during his trip to speak to the Florida State football team with (left to right) FCA representative Doug Scott, then Florida State head coach Bobby Bowden and Dave Van Halanger.

Yo-yo world champion Bunny Martin (center) striking a match from the mouths of Albert (left) and Sam Wyche (right). About 10 years later, Bunny struck a match from the mouth of Albert's son Mike and 10 years after that from the mouth of Albert's grandson Garrett, something that Bunny says is the only three generation family he has ever done that with.

Albert (seated) being roasted in his hometown of Durham, NC in 1986 by (left to right) Richard Bell, John Lotz, Bobby Jones, Danny Lotz, Steve Hale, Lake Speed and Bobby Richardson.

Albert visits with Roger Staubach (middle) during one of his visits to see his son Jeff Staubach (right) play baseball at Duke during the late 1990's.

(Left to right) John Lotz, Albert, former NFL quarterback Gary Cuozzo and former UNC quarterback Mark Maye.

James Jeffrey (far left) with Albert and Barbara and Robin Hayes at an FCA function in 1991 less than four months before the Lord took him home.

(Left to right) John Lotz, Marsha and Don Shinnick, and Albert at Don's FCA Hall of Champions induction in San Diego in 1999.

(Left to right) Bucky Waters, Clyde King, Albert, Clebe McClary and Coach Jerry Moore at an FCA function in Boone, NC.

Happenings Inc. Board members Danny Lotz (far left), Homer Rice (second from left) and Bill Cobey (far right) with Albert.

(Left to right) Mike Kolen, Bobby Richardson, former FCA CEO John Erickson, Albert, former FCA CEO Dal Shealy and former FCA CEO General Dick Abel.

The group that Albert describes as "The Magnificent Seven" includes some of FCA's longest standing supporters and organizers: Back row (left to right) Mike Kolen, Albert and Johnny Hunton; Front row (left to right) Bill Krisher, Danny Lotz, Bobby Richardson and Clebe McClary.

Three generations of Longs in front of Lee Hall at the FCA conference at Black Mountain in 2010: (left to right) Albert, Mike and Garrett.

The Long Family from the fall of 2011: (top row, left to right) Garrett, Caroline, Mike, Kirk and Danny; (bottom row, left to right) Libby, Jackie and Albert.

(Left to right) Bob Bryan, former Major League Baseball pitcher Dave Dravecky and Albert at a FCA banquet.

THE MAN IN THE HAT
God Blesses The Meek

"Blessed are the meek, for they will inherit the earth." – Matthew 5:5 (NIV)

I'm fully aware of what the Bible says about worshipping idols. It's such a big deal to God that it's the first of His Ten Commandments (Exodus 20:3). The closest I've ever come to breaking that rule would be my admiration for the Hall of Fame NFL coach who was known as "the man in the hat."

Tom Landry wasn't an idol in my life, but he was someone that I respected greatly and looked up to as a role model and an example of godliness. I first met Coach Landry at the FCA retreat at Black Mountain in 1966. At that time, he was six years into his career as the head coach for the Dallas Cowboys. In fact, that following season, he was named NFL Coach of the Year.

Coach Landry came back to Black Mountain often and would usually bring his wife Alicia. Even after great success with two Super Bowl championships and five NFC championships, he was always just one of the boys and never showed anything but genuine humility.

After a few years of getting to know him better, he invited me to speak at the Cowboys' pre-game chapel on three separate occasions. Coach Landry was right there every time. I was also thrilled when he agreed to serve on the Advisory Board for my ministry Happenings, Inc.

Rubbing shoulders with Coach Landry was like rubbing shoulders with Billy Graham. He was a man of impeccable integrity. He never compromised his Christian faith. Never!

(Left to right) Coach Joe Gibbs, Coach Tom Landry and Albert
at Charlotte Motor Speedway before a NASCAR race.

But perhaps the one thing that stood out the most was his unmistakable meekness. This isn't the dictionary definition of the word, but some have defined meekness as "strength under control." I can think of no better way to describe Coach Landry. He always had a pleasant, calm demeanor. He was by no means weak. He was truly a powerful man that always kept his emotions from getting the best of him, even in the most pressure packed situations.

Coach Landry's meekness shone through in the way he treated everyone. He truly loved people and showed concern for their wellbeing. Coach Landry also showed his meek, gentle spirit in the way he loved his wife Alicia. The two were married for 51 years until he died of leukemia in 2000.

Coach Landry once signed a picture of the two of us with Joe Gibbs at a NASCAR race in Charlotte and wrote "Romans 8:38-39" next to his autograph. That scripture says this:

"For I am convinced that neither death nor life, neither angels nor demons, neither the present nor the future, nor any powers, neither height nor depth, nor anything else in all creation, will be able to separate us from the love of God that is in Christ Jesus our Lord."

No, Coach Landry wasn't my idol, but I'm so glad I was able to call such a wonderful, living example of meekness my friend. Yes, it was just a coincidence that he was a part of my life. – *AL*

God Blesses The Meek

Coach Tom Landry defied the stereotype of the gruff coach that has to scream and stomp around in order to get results from his players. Others like John Wooden, Tom Osborne, Bobby Bowden and more recently Tony Dungy and Lovie Smith have proven that you can be successful as a coach (and more importantly impact athletes in a positive way) by maintaining a meek approach.

According to the Merriam-Webster dictionary, some synonyms for "meek" are "down-to-earth," "humble," "modest," "unassuming," and "unpretentious." All of those words describe Coach Landry and these other gentlemen perfectly. It might not be easy to display meekness in a society that rewards selfish, boisterous behavior, but Landry knew something about God's economy that we can all benefit from understanding.

In a portion of the New Testament referred to as "The Beatitudes," Jesus taught a sermon that listed several characteristics that go against human nature and social norms but that bring incredible benefits both in this temporal world and in the eternal existence yet to come. One of those teachings spoke specifically to the issue of meekness:

"Blessed are the meek, for they will inherit the earth." – Matthew 5:5 (NIV)

Later on in the New Testament, the Apostle Paul teaches that meekness is one of the fruits of the Spirit (Galatians 5:22-23/KJV). In other words, it is a characteristic that should accompany anyone who is doing his or her best to follow the Holy Spirit in an effort to be like Jesus.

Life Long Lesson
God blesses the meek with His favor and true success.

Unfortunately, the world defines meekness as weakness and too often it seems that only the brash, self-absorbed types ever get anywhere in life. But God sees strength in our meekness. He understands just how difficult it is for humans to resist prideful attitudes and therefore gives favor to those who master the spiritual art of humility.

That doesn't necessarily mean meekness will result in financial wealth, political power, personal popularity or some other measure of worldly success. But it does mean that God will open doors for those who humbly prefer others over themselves as a means by which He can do a work in and through their lives. – *CB*

Going Long

1. Besides coach Tom Landry and the others listed, who are some other leaders that you can name, either well known or someone in your personal life, that exhibit meekness?

2. Why is it so difficult for people to live out the biblical principle of meekness? What are some ways that a lack of meekness might cause problems in today's society?

3. Read Matthew 5:5. In what ways do you think the meek can "inherit the earth?" Can you ever see this principle play out in your life or in the life of someone else?

Today's Prayer: Lord, help me recognize the pride in my life that is keeping me from exercising meekness towards others. Help me to be gracious in both my successes and my failures. Grant me the wisdom to follow Your Spirit. I truly want Your favor to be released in my life.

CHAPTER SEVEN

THE ROLEX WATCH
God Knows The Real You

"… on the outside you appear to people as righteous but on the inside you are full of hypocrisy and wickedness."– Matthew 23:28 *(NIV)*

Not everything is what it appears to be.

That simple statement has been the theme for one of my most effective messages when speaking to groups across the country like Clemson's FCA where I visited for the first time in August of 1975 and returned the next seven years. At the time, Clemson had one of the largest FCA groups in the United States, and still does.

They called the group "9:17" because that's what time they met each week–9:17 p.m. I don't know why it wasn't 9:00 or 9:30. But it was 9:17. About a thousand college students would pack out a gigantic auditorium. Each time I went there, they would allow me to give an invitation. But first, I would close the talk with my Rolex watch story, which goes something like this:

"I've got a Rolex Watch. It is absolutely gorgeous. I've always want- ed a Rolex Watch and I got one and it's beautiful. It's beautiful on the outside, but it's a phony. It's imitation on the inside. I got this Rolex Watch in New York City on the street for fifteen dollars. There are a lot of you out there right now that are just like my Rolex Watch. You know that on the outside, you're beautiful. But you know on the inside, you're an imitation. You're a phony. You know that you need to get your life right with the Lord and you haven't done it. Now, if you've got the guts, and you want to admit that you're phony on the inside and you want to be real for Jesus, I want you to come down right now for prayer."

Every time, kids all over the building would make their way down the aisle to the front. It was always a powerful moment as those college students committed to an authentic relationship with Jesus Christ.

In 1992, about 10 years after my last visit to Clemson, I spoke for the FCA conference at Black Mountain. After I used that same Rolex watch story, a very young college coach made a decision to follow Christ. Some 15 years later, he spoke at Black Mountain in the same auditorium and shared his story. When I learned of his testimony, I immediately found his address and sent him one of my many fifteen-dollar watches.

His name is Warren Belin and he's spent the last several years coaching at places like Cornell, SMU, Vanderbilt and Georgia, most recently at the NFL level as the linebacker coach for the Carolina Panthers. During the summer of 2011, I spoke to Warren and he told me that he used that Rolex story the first time he spoke to the Panthers as a team. He even showed them the watch.

People want to be real with God but sometimes it takes some tough talk to give them the courage to admit that their lives aren't all that they seem to be. Thank you Ed Williams for introducing me to that imitation Rolex and your cousin Louis Mason for sending me the first one I ever used. Yes, it was just a coincidence how the Lord used something like a fake designer watch to touch so many people. – *AL*

God Knows The Real You

When Albert shared his Rolex watch message to those college students at Clemson, he did so understanding the powerful truth behind these words that Jesus spoke some 2,000 years earlier:

"Woe to you, teachers of the law and Pharisees, you hypocrites! You are like whitewashed tombs, which look beautiful on the outside but

on the inside are full of the bones of the dead and everything unclean. In the same way, on the outside you appear to people as righteous but on the inside you are full of hypocrisy and wickedness."
–Matthew 23:27-28 (NIV)

Jesus spent the entire chapter of Matthew 23 exposing the Pharisees' hypocritical ways. These religious leaders of the time would interpret scripture and pass judgment on the people, but were often found to be arrogant and morally bankrupt. It was all about putting on a good show.

Sadly, many Christians in our nation have fallen prey to this pharisaical mindset. While not necessarily spurred by the same set of motivations, pride remains the root cause of hypocrisy in today's church. It's easier to look good on the outside than to actually do the right things. It's easier to play the part than to follow the Spirit. And it goes against human nature to openly admit our shortcomings, our failures and our sins.

Here's the bad news: God knows the real you. He knows you inside out. He knows your heart. He knows your thoughts. God knows if you have truly committed your life to Him or if you are nothing more than a "whitewashed tomb."

But here's the good news: God knows the real you, and He loves you anyway! We know this because of what Jesus did on the Cross:

"But God demonstrates his own love for us in this: While we were still sinners, Christ died for us." – Romans 5:8 (NIV)

The Apostle Paul also writes in Romans 3:23 that "all have sinned and fall short of the glory of God." So it doesn't matter how hypocritical your life is or what sin you might be hiding from others. God knows all about it and He's waiting for the real you to step forward and make a bold, authentic commitment to Jesus. – CB

Life Long Lesson
God knows the real you and He loves you anyway.

Going Long

1. What is your definition of hypocrisy? Can you give some examples?

2. In what areas of your life have you struggled with hypocrisy? Why do you think it's so easy for people to be hypocritical?

3. Have you ever tried to portray yourself as being stronger in your faith than you really were? If so, why did you feel the need to hide your imperfections? What might be some other root causes of hypocritical behavior amongst Christians?

4. Read Romans 5:8. Why is this scripture good news to you personally?

5. Read Romans 3:23. How does this truth help you deal with the temptation to hide your sins and imperfections from God and others?

6. What are some things that you can start doing today that will help you have a more authentic relationship with God and fellow believers?

Today's Prayer: Lord, You know me from the inside out. You see my faults, my failures and my hidden sins. Thank You for loving me anyway! I don't want to be a phony. I want to make an authentic commitment to You today. Give me the strength to be real with You.

CHAPTER EIGHT

NO CREDIT REQUIRED
God Exalts The Humble

"Whoever humbles himself will be exalted." – *Matthew 23:12b*
(NIV)

It's hard to be humble. Our human nature is rooted in pride and it's much easier to toot our own horns rather than let God take care of our promotions in life. That's a valuable lesson that I learned from two outstanding men of God: Calvin Thielman and Stuart Briscoe.

For 33 years, Calvin was the pastor of Montreat Presbyterian Church. Reverend Billy Graham was his most famous member, although you'd never hear Calvin talk about that distinct honor. When he passed away in 2002, I was left with some wonderful memories of the times spent with this humble preacher.

One time in particular comes to mind. One summer during the early years of my ministry, I was returning home from a speaking engagement near Asheville and decided to stop off in Montreat to visit Calvin. He was so good at knowing how to fill my cup.

While there, Calvin mentioned to me that Dr. Stuart Briscoe was down the mountain at Ridgecrest, a popular Baptist conference facility that was hosting a youth retreat. Stuart was one of the guest speakers. At the time, he was already known as a successful pastor, church planter, author and radio minister. Stuart became known for his work at Elmbrook Church in Brookfield, Wisconsin and Torchbearers International.

I had no idea whether or not I could find him at Ridgecrest, but lo and behold, he was standing by himself in the first building I entered. He was gracious to take some time to talk to me outside on the patio. I told him that as a young whippersnapper just getting started, I was using a lot of his material, but I always made sure to give him credit.

When I asked him how he felt about that, he shared with me an interesting story. Stuart told me that not long before our meeting he received a $10 check from *Decision Magazine* for a quote they had used from him. He immediately sent the check to Major Ian Thomas, the person from whom he got the quote, and told him to forward it on to whomever he got the quote.

Stuart then proceeded to tell me that it was not necessary to ever mention his name or give him credit as long as the material was lifting up the Lord and expanding His Kingdom. Believe it or not, many years later, I had some individuals come to me about using my material. I bet you can guess how I answered their question.

Yes, it was just a coincidence that I ran into Stuart Briscoe that day. Through both Stuart and Calvin's influence, I received two living examples of what James preached in his New Testament epistle:

"Humble yourselves before the Lord, and He will lift you up." –
James 4:10 (NIV) – AL

God Exalts The Humble

Sometimes we get caught up in who should get the credit. Maybe that's because in today's world, people are often rewarded for self-promotion while humility seems to get people nowhere. But the Bible has something very different to say about the matter.

First of all, King Solomon shares this ageless nugget of wisdom:

"A man's pride brings him low, but a man of lowly spirit gains honor." – Proverbs 29:23 (NIV)

Men like Calvin Thielman and Stuart Briscoe are prime examples of this principle. Certainly Billy Graham would also fit into the category of the humble leader. Unfortunately, the number of people that can be labeled as such has dwindled considerably as our society has been inundated with humanistic, me-first philosophies.

But as Jesus taught His disciples, there are benefits to humility and consequences to pride:

"For whoever exalts himself will be humbled, and whoever humbles himself will be exalted." – Matthew 23:12 (NIV)

No one was more qualified to teach about humility than the Son of God. He lowered Himself to become man, to walk the earth and ultimately to die for the sins of the world. And in the end, Jesus was exalted and continues to be exalted above all things. He knew His purpose and never allowed the sin of pride to keep Him from obeying His Father's will.

And that principle holds true for us today. As Peter noted in his letter to the early Church, God can do some amazing things in our lives when we walk with humility.

"Humble yourselves, therefore, under God's mighty hand, that he may lift you up in due time." – 1 Peter 5:6 (NIV)

When we let pride drive our pursuits, we often get ahead of God's plan for our lives. Any success we experience will be built on a shaky foundation. And when we can point to what we did to make it happen, we take the glory away from Him. But when we put our pride aside, we exalt God who in turn blesses our faithfulness and places us in the center of His will. – *CB*

> **Life Long Lesson**
> **When you're tempted to give in to your prideful nature, remember that God exalts the humble and will fulfill His purpose for you in His timing.**

Going Long

1. What are some common occurrences in life where people are eager to get the credit for doing something good or noteworthy? What do you think typically drives that desire?

2. Can you think of some instances where you should have gotten credit for something but it was given to someone else or not given at all? If so, how did that challenge your pride?

3. Albert talks about two men who weren't concerned about recognition or credit. Is it really possible to get ahead in today's society by practicing humility like that? Explain.

4. Go back and read all three passages mentioned in this chapter. How do they challenge you and your personal struggle with pride and humility? How do they encourage and strengthen you?

5. What are some things that you can start doing today that will help you not worry so much about getting credit and allowing God to sort those things out for the advancement of your future?

Today's Prayer: Lord, search my heart and reveal to me any impure motives as it relates to seeking out credit and recognition for the good things that I may do. Help me to understand and truly believe the fact that You have my best interest in heart and that You will promote me in due time.

CHAPTER NINE

THE ULTIMATE PARDON
God's Grace Overcomes All Sin

"If we confess our sins, he is faithful and just and will forgive us our sins and purify us from all unrighteousness." – 1 John 1:9 (NIV)

There are many lessons we can learn from observing the godly lives of others. But sometimes, the most powerful example comes by watching how people respond to their failures.

And then there's Loren Young, someone who exemplified what it looks like to walk in grace on both accounts.

Loren was one of my favorite people from the moment I met him at an FCA conference at Black Mountain back in the mid-60s. He was a talented quarter-miler for Duke's track team and coincidentally used to watch Durham High School's football games when I was playing there. Loren always talked about seeing "Long and Lutz" during our back-to-back undefeated seasons. When he did, I always told him to put Worth Lutz (who went on to play quarterback at Duke) ahead of me because he was "all everything."

After finishing his undergraduate work, Loren joined the FCA staff in Durham and later spent several years as the Southeastern Regional Director. He was always by far the most popular speaker at the conferences at Black Mountain and Rome, Georgia.

Loren once shared a saying with me that I then used at every one of my school assembly speaking engagements. My son Mike also used it in his video "Everyone Is NOT Doing It." The saying goes like this:

"If I love you I will never hurt you. I will never use you, nor will I ever abuse you, and you will be a better person, because I love you."

In his later years, he made a terrible mistake that resulted in a lengthy prison sentence. Thanks to Harold Morris, author of *Twice Pardoned*, Loren was granted an early release about four years later. But perhaps the greatest heartbreak was how so many of his old friends, that more or less idolized him, immediately departed from him because of what he did. My good friend John Lotz and myself, along with a few others, were among a small group that refused to abandon Loren during this dark time in his life.

After he was released, Loren found a job at Hilton Head, South Carolina as a security guard where he earned just a little over minimum wage. When John was in assisted living here in Durham and struggling with his cancer, Loren drove an old car up from Hilton Head three different times to visit his dear friend. He stayed with my wife Jackie and me all three times.

There is absolutely no doubt in my mind that he had repented from his sin and was a new creature in Christ. I'd like for any of you, who departed from him that might be reading this book, to read that sentence over again. I am convinced that Loren certainly understood and lived out this powerful scripture:

"If we confess our sins, he is faithful and just and will forgive us our sins and purify us from all unrighteousness." – 1 John 1:9 (NIV)

And as the apostle Paul wrote in 2 Corinthians 5:17, Loren was a brand new creation. I'm so thankful that God doesn't just forgive. He forgets. He erases the board. He destroys the evidence. He burns the microfilm. He clears the computer.

In 2003, Loren died shortly after John had passed. Harold Morris found his body in his apartment probably three days after he had died, all alone. What a tragedy.

It was just a coincidence that Loren Young played such a large part in my life. I'm thankful that the Lord arranged for me to meet Loren at Black Mountain and even more thankful that God forgave him of his sin and restored him back to a relationship with Him. Loren is proof that no sin is greater than the blood of Jesus and God's amazing grace. – *AL*

God's Grace Overcomes All Sin

It was truly a blessing when Loren Young received an early release from prison. Although his life would never be the same, he was at least able to enjoy his personal freedom and work to restore his place in society.

But the ultimate pardon came when Loren asked God to forgive him of his sin. He leaned on the truth found in 1 John 1:9 and allowed the Lord to not just forgive him, but also to purify him from unrighteousness.

The Bible provides many other stories of how God's grace overcomes all sin. In the Old Testament, King David's disobedient behavior is well chronicled and often cited as one of history's most redemptive stories. In 2 Samuel 11, we read about how his lust for a married woman led to adultery and ultimately murder. Like Loren, David paid a price for his sin but was ultimately restored back to a relationship with God.

In the New Testament, we have another great example in the life of Paul. As a religious zealot named Saul, he terrorized the early Christians and was even present when Stephen became the first recorded martyr. But in Acts 9, we read about Paul's miraculous conversion. Perhaps no one was better equipped to write these words than the Apostle himself:

"Therefore, if anyone is in Christ, the new creation has come: The old has gone, the new is here!" – 2 Corinthians 5:17 (NIV)

Perhaps you have committed a sin that seems too awful for God to forgive. Or maybe you're having trouble forgiving someone else who has done something terribly wrong to you or someone you love. In both cases, there is much freedom in understanding how our Creator deals with these issues. He forgives those who repent and He gives them a brand new start.

That is the essence of God's amazing grace–the ultimate pardon. – *CB*

Life Long Lesson
No matter the circumstance, God's grace overcomes all sin, renews all sinners and restores them back to Him.

Going Long

1. What are some sins that are often considered unforgivable in today's society? Do you think there are any sins that we should forgive? Explain.

2. Loren Young lived an exemplary life for God but a horrible mistake in his later years tarnished his reputation and even caused some of his friends to abandon him. Can you think of another situation like this? What do you think these kinds of stories tell us about the importance of living consistent, godly lives?

3. Read 1 John 1:9. According to this scripture, what should we do when we sin? What are the things that God does in response? How does this scripture impact the way you view others who have sinned and yourself in times when you have sinned?

4. Read 2 Corinthians 5:17. For you personally, what is the significance of this scripture? Does it impact your ability to forgive others who have done wrong? Does it impact your ability to forgive yourself for past mistakes?

5. Do you have any sins for which you need to ask God's forgiveness? Is there someone in your life that you have not forgiven for something hurtful they did? If so, read the prayer below and begin walking in God's grace.

Today's Prayer: Lord, forgive me of my sins. I repent and turn from my old ways. Give me the strength to walk in Your grace and to embrace the new creation that I have become. And help me to forgive others that have hurt me or done things that caused me to lose trust in them. Give me the compassion to reach out and help them through the difficulties they are facing.

CHAPTER TEN

THE PIANO MAN
God Desires Your Availability

"Then I heard the voice of the Lord saying, 'Whom shall I send? And who will go for us?' And I said, 'Here am I. Send me!" – Isaiah 6:8 *(NIV)*

You can have all the talent in the world, but it won't make much of a difference if you aren't willing to make yourself available to God. That's something I learned through the example of a man named Randy Atcheson.

I first met Randy during that summer of 1972 at the Black Mountain FCA retreat. His brother Wayne Atcheson was the state director for Alabama at the time and organized the event.

Wayne came to me and said, "Albert, you're in for a treat today. I've got my brother with me."

And I said, "Oh really? What's he gonna do?"

"He plays piano," Wayne replied.

I couldn't resist the opportunity to crack a joke.

"Oh yeah? Is he gonna play chop sticks?"

Wayne came back at me and said, "Yeah, you wait until you hear his chop sticks."

Well, Wayne was right. His brother was absolutely incredible. I'd never heard anything like it, and he was just playing an old upright. We didn't have a grand piano at Black Mountain. Randy would later become the first person to receive a double major from Juilliard School of Music. He majored in both piano *and* organ.

Later that night, we stood in front of Lee Hall and I told the young musician about my desire to became an evangelist:

"Randy, the Lord has anointed me. I don't know what He's got in mind. But it looks like He's trying to take me out of the insurance business and have me start a ministry. If it ever works out, I wonder if I could get you a plane ticket and have you join me."

I'll never forget his answer.

"Albert, if you get me out of New York, I'll come anywhere just for expenses."

Neither of us realized at that moment that he would become a member of the Happenings team a couple of years later and be with us for the entire 25 years that followed. He also didn't know that he would eventually travel all over the world as a concert pianist and perform in Carnegie Hall more than 10 times. His most recent appearance was November of 2012 and I was right there cheering him on, especially when he played "Amazing Grace" like he always does for his first encore.

Randy has blessed many lives with his great talent, but I know that God is most pleased with him because of his consistent openness to be used. That's really what God desires from all of us. Yes, it was just a coincidence that I met such a talented young man at Black Mountain and learned a lesson about availability through his example. – *AL*

God Desires Your Availability

Not everyone is musically gifted like Randy Atcheson or even athletically talented enough to letter in four collegiate sports like Albert did at the University of North Carolina. But everyone has God-given abilities.

Some people are artistic. Some people are skilled in math or sciences. Some people are good teachers. Some people are good listeners. Some people are adept at financial matters. Some people are naturally kind and generous.

There is one gift, however, that everyone shares–time. No matter what our level of ability in any given discipline or what our personality traits might be, the greatest thing we can give God is our availability.

In the Old Testament, the prophet Isaiah wrestled with the idea that God could use him. How could a man with no great distinction do anything significant for the Creator of the universe? Finally, Isaiah realized that God was simply looking for someone who was willing to obey His commands and fulfill His calling.

"Whom shall I send? And who will go for us?'" the Lord asked. "Here am I. Send me!" Isaiah famously replied. (Isaiah 6:8/NIV)

We too can feel incompetent, unprepared and simply not good enough to do anything for God. All of those things are true. We aren't competent, prepared or good enough to do God's will–at least not on our own. But as the oft-quoted phrase says, "God doesn't call the equipped. He equips the called."

And when we're not feeling up to the task at hand, just remember how overwhelmed the disciples felt when Jesus told them they would soon be carrying on His work without Him. Understanding their human weakness and doubt, Jesus shared these words of encouragement:

"But the Advocate, the Holy Spirit, whom the Father will send in my name, will teach you all things and will remind you of everything I have said to you." – John 14:26 (NIV)

God wants you to share His love and the message of salvation and hope with the world. But it's up to you to be available to His call. Don't worry about how you're going to do it. Just trust that He will equip you with everything you need to get the job done. – *CB*

> **Life Long Lesson**
> **God desires your availability**
> **and will equip you to do His work.**

Going Long

1. What are some talents and abilities upon which we tend to place a high value? Why do you think that's the case?

2. What are some other talents and abilities that aren't as celebrated? In your opinion, are they less valuable, more valuable or equally valuable in God's eyes?

3. What are some things that have made you hesitant to answer God's call? Have you overcome those issues? Explain. If not, what's holding you back?

4. What do you feel like God is calling you to do? Read John 14:26. How do Jesus' words to His disciples encourage and empower you in your situation?

5. What are some things that you can begin doing today that will help you step out and begin to accept the calling that God gave Isaiah and continues to give to His followers today?

Today's Prayer: Lord, give me the strength to overcome my fears, my self-doubt and my inadequacies. I know that you have gifted me with certain talents and abilities and I want to use them for Your glory and for the expansion of Your Kingdom. I want to make myself available to You. Here I am, Lord. Send me.

CHAPTER ELEVEN

ROYAL TREATMENT
God Delights In Our Kindness

"Therefore, as we have opportunity, let us do good to all people, especially to those who belong to the family of believers." – Galatians 6:10 (NIV)

True kindness never plays favorites. No one better modeled that principle than Bill Wade.

As a senior quarterback at Vanderbilt, Bill was an All-American and SEC Most Valuable Player. He went on to have a successful 13-year pro career with the Los Angeles Rams and the Chicago Bears. In 1963, Bill led the Bears to the NFL Championship against the New York Giants and legendary quarterback Y.A. Tittle. In eight-degree weather at Wrigley Field, he scored both of Chicago's touchdowns in a 14-10 victory.

I first met Bill that next year at Black Mountain. You would have never known that he was an NFL champion and two-time Pro Bowl selection. Bill would always lead the guys three quarters of a mile up the steep hill from the intramural fields carrying a cross and singing "Onward Christians Soldiers." It was quite a sight to see.

But it was another memory of Bill, three or four years later at a citywide FCA event in Nashville, Tennessee, that really showed my wife Jackie and me such a special example of kindness. At the reception, we walked into a large room as total strangers to most of the people that were present. When Bill saw us standing by ourselves, he immediately walked away from the dignitaries he was with and welcomed us like we were the King and Queen of England.

Bill was a representation of Jesus that evening. Our Lord never concerned Himself with the high falootin' people. He always spent time with "the least of these." So following Bill's example, I made up my mind that if I ever became a featured speaker in the future, I would always introduce myself to anyone there who was a stranger. Yes, it was just a coincidence that I met Bill Wade at Black Mountain back in 1964 and then later learned such an important lesson about kindness from him in Nashville. And by the way, I still follow his example today. Thank you Bill. – *AL*

God Delights In Our Kindness

When Bill Wade saw Albert and Jackie in that room in Nashville, he immediately recognized how out of place they must have felt. So he walked away from the more important people and gave the relative strangers the royal treatment.

Of course, when we study the Bible, we see that in God's eyes there really is no such thing as people that are more or less important. The Apostle Peter learned this truth in Acts 10 when he was introduced to a man named Cornelius, a Roman centurion who was a devout Christian. But this was in a time when the converted Jews were still struggling to accept the fact that Jesus had also come to save the Gentiles. So God gave Peter a vision (Acts 10:9-23) to help him see the truth.

"I now realize how true it is that God does not show favoritism but accepts from every nation the one who fears him and does what is right." – Acts 10:34-35 (NIV)

We might not have those same types of prejudices when it comes to salvation, but as humans, we sometimes get caught up in the concept of status or even likeability. It's easier to be kind to someone who can give us something in return or to someone who has a pleasant personality.

But the Apostle Paul reminds us in his letter to the church at Galatia that we have a much greater responsibility.

"Therefore, as we have opportunity, let us do good to all people, especially to those who belong to the family of believers." – *Galatians 6:10 (NIV)*

He reiterated this point in another familiar passage but added an interesting twist:

"Don't neglect to show hospitality, for by doing this some have welcomed angels as guests without knowing it." – *Hebrews 13:2 (HCSB)*

Like Albert said, Jesus spent most of his time showing love and kindness to the so-called unimportant members of society. So the next time you see someone who seems sad, lonely or out of place, remember that God delights in our kindness to others (Jeremiah 9:35)–especially those who need it the most. – *CB*

Life Long Lesson
God delights in our kindness to all people,
especially those who need it the most.

Going Long

1. In general, to which types of people is it most difficult to show kindness? Is that also true for you? Explain.

2. Why do you think it's usually easier to be kind to others deemed more important by society's standards? What do you think this says about our culture and the concept of "favoritism?"

3. Think about Jesus' life on earth. What are some examples of how He showed kindness to people that others might have overlooked? Who are the people in today's world that Jesus would likely reach out to with his love and kindness?

4. Read Galatians 6:10 and Hebrews 13:2. What do these scriptures mean to you?

5. What are some ways that you can start to live out all of these passages and begin showing kindness to others today?

Today's Prayer: Lord, teach me out to show kindness to others. Overflow my heart with Your perfect love so that I might recognize when others are lonely or hurting and could use a kind word or action.

CHAPTER TWELVE

BROTHERLY ADVICE
Godly Correction Eases Conflict

"I myself am convinced, my brothers and sisters, that you yourselves are full of goodness, filled with knowledge and competent to instruct one another." – Romans 15:14 (NIV)

There's a right way and a wrong way to deal with conflict inside the Body of Christ. I learned that very serious lesson from a very funny man.

I first met Grady Nutt at Black Mountain in the early 1970s. Grady always attended the summer FCA conferences in Rome, Georgia, as well, and through those events we became close friends.

In 1979, we had a banquet in Durham for the purpose of introducing people to Happenings, Inc. Grady came in from Kentucky just to emcee the event. That was the same year he was added to the regular cast of "Hee Haw." He was already a popular commodity in the church community, but now his career as a comedian, actor, recording artist and author was really starting to take off on a much larger scale.

It's a little known fact that Grady was also an outstanding photographer. When I found out about his picture-taking skills, I asked him if he would take our family portrait. That experience was a blast. The photo turned out great because he had all of us so relaxed the entire time. I think it was one of only two times I ever saw him so serious. The other time had a much more profound impact on my life.

I don't recall the exact date, but it was somewhere in the mid-1970s. I had received a couple of calls from friends who had been

The one and only Grady Nutt—a dear friend and one who let his light shine for our great Lord everywhere he went.

trying to get Grady to speak at their events. Both parties mentioned they couldn't afford his expensive booking fee. So what did this young know-it-all evangelist do? I wrote my friend Grady a letter. I wrote to him about the two phone calls and then had the audacity to quote Luke 12:48: "To whom much is given, much is required in return."

Nothing came of it until we both arrived in Rome, Georgia for an FCA conference. Grady saw me check into the hotel and asked me if I had a minute. I did, of course, and we drove down the road to Shoney's. As we sat opposite each other, I'll never forget what he had to say:

"I know you were an outstanding four sport athlete at UNC, and we have been friends in the Lord for many years now," he said. "But I want you to listen to what I have to say. Don't interrupt me until I have finished what I want to say or I'll wrap these hands around your neck and wring it."

On a side note, Grady had the unusual talent of "playing his hands," but I wasn't thinking about that during this particular conversation.

"I want you to know that I have spoken at more Valentine banquets, and more churches, than you will ever speak at," Grady continued. "I've heard 'God bless you brother, I'll pray for your journey back home,'" when all I would have liked was a little gas money more times than you ever will. Now, the good Lord has blessed me to the point that my services are more in demand than any time in my life. This has provided financial security for my family. I now have a calendar for each day of the year that I am willing to leave my wife and family. When my allotted days are full, that's it, regardless of who calls. Then I get a letter like yours from a supposed brother in Christ who has no idea in the world about my situation. Listen to me Albert, and don't you ever forget this. When you want to admonish a brother, or anyone, as far as that goes, don't you ever write a letter. If you are unable to meet him face to face, you call him on the phone and discuss it."

He added a few more things, like only Grady could do, until we both were crying and walking out of Shoney's with our arms wrapped around each other. I have failed with that advice only once since and that was from an email I sent a friend. We straightened it out immediately.

On November 23, 1982, I was in South Carolina for a "Happening" event. Early the next morning, something on the radio downstairs woke me up. I jumped out of my bed and asked my host, "Did I just hear something about Grady Nutt?

That's when I learned of the tragedy. The night before, Grady and his two pilots were killed after a chartered flight out of Cullman, Alabama, crashed right after take-off. He was 48 years old. I cried like a baby.

Most people will always remember Grady for his humor. I certainly will remember that too. But I'm most thankful for the coincidence that allowed me to learn that invaluable lesson about dealing with disagreements and conflict amongst the brethren. I'm forever grateful to Grady for that great piece of brotherly advice. – *AL*

Godly Correction Eases Conflict

One of the biggest problems we often face within the Body of Christ is conflict resolution. Fellow Christians sometimes disagree on biblical issues, have differing views on practical matters or even struggle to properly deal with sinful behavior inside the church walls.

For Albert and Grady, the conflict started when Albert made some wrong assumptions based on incomplete information. He compounded the problem by writing Grady a letter instead of discussing the matter with him in person or over the phone. It was a humbling lesson that forever changed Albert's approach to correction.

Certainly, Grady brought wisdom from God's Word to that fateful meeting. As a seminary graduate and minister, he was well aware of Paul's writings on the importance of peer-to-peer counsel and instruction:

"Let the message of Christ dwell among you richly as you teach and admonish one another with all wisdom through psalms, hymns, and songs from the Spirit, singing to God with gratitude in your hearts."
– *Colossians 3:16 (NIV)*

Grady also had a firm grasp of how to specifically handle a dispute between Christian brothers or how to deal with sins or other grievances with the church community. That's because Jesus had laid it out in His teachings to the disciples:

"If your brother or sister sins, go and point out their fault, just between the two of you. If they listen to you, you have won them over." - Matthew 18:15 (NIV)

Certainly, Grady had won Albert over by the end of their conversation and displayed the power of Godly correction and Spirit-led counsel. As Albert said, it's a lesson he will never forget and one that he has never failed to implement since. - *CB*

Life Long Lesson
When another brother or sister in Christ has erred in their ways, remember that Godly correction eases conflict and works towards resolving the situation.

Going Long

1. What are some conflicts that might come up within a church community or between followers of Christ? Have you ever experienced any of these types of conflicts?

2. When you've had to deal with conflict amongst the brethren, what are some ways that you handled it? Which ways turned out well and which ways turned out poorly? Can you explain those results?

3. Read Colossians 3:16. What are some of the benefits that might come from adhering to the advice given in this passage? Have you personally experienced any of those benefits? Have you ever been negatively impacted because this teaching was ignored?

4. Read Matthew 18:15-17. Take a look at verse 15 and discuss the importance of one-on-on discussions at the beginning of a conflict.

Now look at verses 16 and 17. Why do you think Jesus teaches that a line must eventually be drawn when correction fails to yield positive results?

5. If you are currently facing an ongoing conflict, look back over Matthew 18:15-17 and prayerfully consider using Jesus' teaching to resolve the matter. When future conflicts arise, remember that passage and the example from Albert and Grady's story as a template for how to proceed.

Today's Prayer: Lord, when conflict between myself and a brother or sister in Christ comes my way, help me to not rush to judgment, but rather to use these New Testament teachings as my guide. Give me wisdom so that I can avoid adding to the problem and instead to be a part of the solution.

CHAPTER THIRTEEN

TAKE IT OR MAKE IT
God Calls us to Evangelize Our World

"...Always be prepared to give an answer to everyone who asks you to give the reason for the hope that you have..." - 1 Peter 3:15 *(NIV)*

"When the opportunity comes, take it. If the opportunity doesn't come, make it."

I first heard that phrase from Dr. Stuart Briscoe and I've used it many times through my ministry. I can't think of anyone who has better lived it out than Fisher DeBerry. Fisher was probably the finest Christian college football coach I ever met, and that's not taking anything away from Bobby Bowden or Fred Goldsmith.

Fisher coached 37 years but is best known for his time as the head coach at the United States Air Force Academy from 1984 to 2006 where he compiled a 169-109-1 record. Fisher led the Falcons to one of its greatest eras of success including 12 bowl game appearances and three Western Athletic Conference titles. He was inducted into the College Football Hall of Fame in 2011.

When Fisher was still the head coach, I used to worry him and his long-time assistant coach Richard Bell to death about getting me out to the Air Force Academy in Colorado Springs to speak at a Sunday service. Each time I talked to them, or wrote them, I would always say something like, "Well, I sure hope you arrange to have me out there before the rapture comes."

Finally, in February of 2004, I got the opportunity. It was such a thrill just to see that gorgeous chapel much less get to speak to the cadets. However, there was one unusual thing that happened. Both Fisher and Richard were not even there that weekend to hear me preach. Richard had a high school reunion back in Arkansas and Fisher was speaking at a big coaches clinic outside the state. Gary Lydic took me on a tour of Focus On The Family the next day. I also got to visit with Dave Dravecky and had a fantastic dinner that night with my old UNC teammate Bill Kirkman.

Fisher returned on Monday and took me around the academy to see everything there. When he asked me about my message to the cadets, I told him it was about the Apostle Paul's boldness then I shared that quote about opportunity. Fisher asked me to write it down for him. About a week later, he had it printed onto a banner and hung up in the team's locker room.

Fisher was a lot like Paul in many regards. He was bold in his witness and never failed to take the opportunity to share the Gospel with others. Also like Paul, he came under a great deal of pressure for his public stand and even had to make some changes in how he approached his Christian faith within the locker room. But Fisher never compromised who he was and always stood strong no matter how difficult things were for him.

It was just a coincidence that I met Fisher and Richard many years ago through FCA and later was blessed to share that message at the Air Force Academy. I'm so thankful for Fisher's example as a modern day Paul and someone who was never afraid to evangelize his world. – *AL*

God Calls Us To Evangelize Our World

"Therefore go and make disciples of all nations, baptizing them in the name of the Father and of the Son and of the Holy Spirit, and teaching them to obey everything I have commanded you. And surely I am with you always, to the very end of the age." – Matthew 28:19-20 (NIV)

It is not insignificant to note that Jesus' final charge to His disciples emphasized evangelism. By following that command, those men changed the world forever. But the call to share the Gospel with others didn't stop with that small group of men. As followers of Christ, we too are called to make new disciples and add souls to God's Kingdom.

In order for us to successfully operate as modern day Apostles, we should be prepared to recognize and take opportunities for evangelism that come our way. They might pop up while standing in the checkout line, working at the office, hanging out at the coffee shop or taking a walk in the neighborhood. And when there are no obvious opportunities around us, we should be willing to boldly make or create them.

Paul modeled this throughout his ministry and encouraged us to do the same:

"...Always be prepared to give an answer to everyone who asks you to give the reason for the hope that you have." - 1 Peter 3:15 (NIV)

Fisher DeBerry used his platform to follow Jesus' command in Matthew 28:19-20. Albert has done the same through ministries such as FCA, Teen Crusade and Happenings, Inc. Most of us might not have those same opportunities, but we are called to evangelize *our* world no matter how big or how small. What matters most is how we *choose* to respond. - *CB*

Life Long Lesson
God calls us to evangelize our world, therefore, always look to make or take opportunities to share the Gospel.

Going Long

1. What does this phrase mean to you: "When the opportunity

comes, take it. If the opportunity doesn't come, make it." Can you describe a time in your life when you took an opportunity that came along? Can you think of a time when you created an opportunity for yourself?

2. Read Matthew 18:19-20. Why do you think this was the last thing Jesus told His disciples before He ascended into Heaven?

3. What are the different commands listed in Matthew 18:19-20? On a scale of 1-10 (1 being easiest, 10 being most difficult), how would you rank the difficulty of following each of those commands?

4. Read 1 Peter 3:15. What do you think it looks like to "be prepared?" What are some opportunities to share the Gospel that might come up in your life? What are some situations where you might be able to make opportunities to lead others to Christ?

5. What are some things that are keeping you from being more bold and active as a modern day apostle of the Christian faith?

Today's Prayer: Lord, give me the courage to boldly proclaim Your Gospel to those in my world and to others that I might meet on a daily basis. I want to be like the Apostle Paul, unafraid and unashamed to share my testimony with people who desperately need to hear about Your unconditional love, Your saving grace and Your promise of eternal life.

CHAPTER FOURTEEN

A CITY ON A HILL
God Calls Us To Shine Our Light

"Let your light shine before others, that they may see your good deeds and glorify your Father in heaven." – Matthew 5:16 (NIV)

Everyone has a circle of influence or a part of the world that can be impacted with the Gospel. In Matthew 5:14-16, Jesus described it as "a city on a hill," and taught His disciples to let their "light shine before others."

No one better lived out this principle than my good friend Ed Britton.

It was back in 1983 when Ed was skimming through an FCA *Sharing the Victory* magazine and checking out a list of audiocassettes that featured available speakers. He noticed that one of the speakers was "the only four sport letterman in ACC history" and ordered my tape. After listening to it, he contacted me and invited me to speak at his son's sports banquet in Virginia. Ed opened up his home to me that night and our friendship quickly developed.

His youngest son Dan, the one at the sports banquet, would later go to the University of Delaware where he was an outstanding lacrosse player. In 1991, Dan began working for FCA, and in 2002 moved to Kansas City with his family to join FCA's National Support Center staff. He is still serving as a vice president for that organization today.

It's clear where Dan picked up his strong desire to serve in the ministry. Ed set an incredible example as the chairman of the Christian Business Men's Committee in Washington D.C., for 32 years. He invited me to speak to that group on two separate occasions and one of those times invited my dear friend Senator Jesse Helms to introduce me. Ed was also one of the founding board members of the Northern Virginia FCA.

Ed helped co-found the Metropolitan Washington Airport Interfaith Chapels, Inc., which today is served by five chaplains. He attended Immanuel Bible Church for 27 years and played a big role in establishing the tract ministry there.

On a personal note, I'm thankful for the example Ed set for me as a member of the Happenings Inc., Advisory Board. As a highly qualified financial expert, he provided a real answer to prayer for Jackie and me when he put together my retirement plan.

In 2006, Ed was diagnosed with leukemia. He bravely fought the cancer the next two years but was never afraid of death. Ed had been an incredible light to the world and took that evangelistic spirit all the way to his hospice care. He still had his container with the tracks nearby and was ready to witness at a moment's notice. Ed's nurses joked that they were sometimes fearful of visiting with him knowing that he was likely going to preach to them all day. He passed away in 2008.

My good friend Ray Hildebrand wrote a song entitled "A Special Kind of Man." I think the good Lord was thinking about Ed the first time He heard Ray sing it. Ed's bust is in FCA's "Hall of Champions." I am so honored that mine is right next to his.

It was just a coincidence that Ed Britton found me in that FCA magazine. I'm so thankful for the light that he shined into my life and into the lives of so many others. – *AL*

God Calls Us To Shine Our Light

Ed Britton was the epitome of the "light" that Jesus called His followers to shine into the world. It didn't matter if it was in the church, in the business world, in the community or within the confines of sports ministry, Ed took that call very seriously and carried it all the way to the end of his time on earth.

Albert has already alluded to this scripture, but let's take a look at the entire passage for its full context:

> "*You are the light of the world. A city on a hill cannot be hidden. Neither do people light a lamp and put it under a bowl. Instead they put it on its stand, and it gives light to everyone in the house. In the same way, let your light shine before men, that they may see your good deeds and praise your Father in heaven.*" *– Matthew 5:14-16 (NIV)*

Once we accept Christ into our hearts, we should have a burning desire to share our experience and His saving power with those around us. Each circle of influence is different in size and scope. Some people might have the opportunity to share God's love with thousands, even millions. But most people are afforded a smaller circle of influence that includes family members, co-workers, neighbors and friends.

There are people all around that need to hear the Gospel message of hope and eternal life that comes through a blood-bought relationship with Jesus. Throughout His ministry, the Savior reminded His disciples of the great need for everyday evangelists to make a difference in the lives of those around them.

> "*The harvest is plentiful but the workers are few. Ask the Lord of the harvest, therefore, to send out workers into his harvest field.*" *– Matthew 5:37-38 (NIV)*

We can be the answer to that prayer. We can be the ones to take up the mantle and become modern day apostles who are willing to share the Gospel with others through word and through deed. We can be the light that Jesus has called to shine into this world. *– CB*

Life Long Lesson
God calls us to shine our light into a world that desperately
needs to hear about His love.

Going Long

1. Go back and read Matthew 5:14-16. How would you rewrite that scripture to reflect the world you live in?

2. Think about your circle of influence. Who are the people that you personally interact with on a regular basis?

3. Go back and read Matthew 5:37-38. Why do you think that, "the workers are few?" Do any of those reasons ever impact your enthusiasm about evangelizing your circle of influence?

4. What are some ways that you can "let your light shine" to the people you see regularly and those with which you might interact through random daily tasks? (Think of specific things that reflect how both your words and your deeds or actions can impact others for the sake of His Kingdom.)

Today's Prayer: Lord, give me the courage and boldness to let my light shine for You. Renew my passion for the lost so that I might impact my circle of influence for Your glory.

CHAPTER FIFTEEN

TRIUMPH OVER TRAGEDY
God Turns Defeats Into Victories

"...we also glory in our sufferings, because we know that suffering produces perseverance; perseverance, character; and character, hope."
– Romans 5:3-4 (NIV)

God always has a way of placing remarkable people in our lives so we can learn from them. For me, one of those people was Dave Dravecky. I met him because of his success as a Major League pitcher, but I learned a valuable lesson from him because of the way he handled defeat.

Dave was an outstanding left-handed pitcher. In his second season, he won 14 games and represented the Padres at the 1983 All-Star game. He was a big part of San Diego's first pennant the following year. Dave joined the Giants midway through the 1987 season and pitched in the National League playoffs where the team lost to the Cardinals. Roger Craig, one of my best friends from Durham High School, was managing San Francisco at the time and introduced me to this rising star.

In 1988, Dave received some tragic news. A cancerous tumor was found in his pitching arm. In October, doctors removed half of his deltoid muscle and then informed Dave that he would never throw a baseball again. During that time, when he had to be at an all-time low, John Lotz and I would call him at least once a month to encourage him.

We didn't realize it at the time, but an absolute miracle was taking place in Dave's life. A few months after his surgery, Dave started to throw the ball around and even later started pitching again.

By July 1989, he was back in the minor leagues where he pitched three games. And then the real miracle took place for the man that doctors said would never throw a baseball again. On August 10, the Giants called Dave up and gave him the start against Cincinnati. He pitched eight innings that day and beat the Reds 4-3 in front of a sellout home crowd. I'll never forget when Roger called me from the clubhouse after the game and said, "Well, your boy did it!"

My wife Jackie and I along with our good friends Bob and Jerry Bryan decided to travel to Montreal to watch him make his next start five days later. Before the game, Bob and I had our picture taken in the stands with Dave warming up in the background. Everything was going great until the sixth inning. After giving up a leadoff homerun and hitting Andres Galarraga with a pitch, Dave faced off against Tim Raines. On the first pitch, his humerus bone snapped and he fell to the mound. You could have heard a pin drop in that stadium.

Dave stayed with the team the rest of the season and cheered them on to the National League pennant. After the Giants beat the Cubs in the playoffs, he broke his arm a second time while running to the field during the celebration. When he had x-rays taken, the doctors discovered that his cancer had returned. Dave's career was over and on June 18, 1991, he had his left arm and shoulder amputated.

I was always amazed at what God was doing through Dave even when he knew he'd never throw a ball again. Every time we called him, he'd be laughing and we'd have a good time. He was so determined he was going to beat it. I'll never forget his determination. His will to continue life in an ordinary way was strong. Even after the surgery, Dave had that same determination. He played golf. He went fly-fishing. How do you do those things with one arm? It was incredible.

As a motivational speaker and author of two books, Dave has made a big impact on many people with his story. Who would have ever thought that 21 years later, Johnny Evans, our FCA regional director, would invite Dave to be the featured speaker in Raleigh for the annual Triangle Banquet? That night, Bob and I had our picture made with him as he held the picture that was taken in Montreal. Yes, it was just a coincidence that the good Lord arranged for me to have such a great friendship with Dave Dravecky–a friendship that I will always treasure. – *AL*

God Turns Defeats Into Victories

Unless you've personally experienced tragedy, it's often difficult to understand what it's like for others who might be dealing with seriously hard times. As Albert watched Dave deal with cancer, a career-ending injury and the unfathomable event that led to the loss of an arm, he and so many onlookers were amazed at the perseverance he displayed.

After Dave's first surgery, God gave him the strength to pitch again–even if for a short time. In hindsight, it's clear to see that this last opportunity to shine on the national stage was part of a bigger plan that God had for his life. And after Dave's amputation, the Lord again gave him strength to overcome the physical and mental anguish and to ultimately find new purpose beyond baseball. He allowed God to turn an awful defeat into an incredible comeback victory.

The Bible tells us about a young man named Joseph who went through a very different set of circumstances that were nonetheless tragic. Already known to be Jacob's favorite son, Joseph became the unfortunate target of his 11 brothers' jealous rage when their father's gift to Joseph, a special multi-colored coat, collectively pushed them over the edge. After throwing him in a pit and conspiring to kill him, the brothers instead decided to sell him into slavery (see Genesis 37).

Joseph ended up in Egypt and was sold to an influential man

named Potiphar. There, things turned around for Joseph and he was promoted to a position of prominence. But his life took another tragic turn when he rejected Potiphar's wife advances. The scorned woman accused Joseph of rape and he was thrown into prison (see Genesis 39:1-23). While there, he interpreted dreams for two fellow prisoners and one of them, the chief cup bearer, was later released and promised he would mention him to Pharaoh. But the man never followed through on that commitment (see Genesis 40:1-23).

Finally, after two years in prison, Joseph was called upon to help the Pharaoh with his troubling dreams. His successful interpretations, indicating that Egypt would have seven years of plenty followed by seven years of famine, vaulted him to an important position within the kingdom. In just a few years time, Joseph went from slave to savior (see Genesis 41).

Despite betrayal, false accusation, imprisonment and abandonment, Joseph remained true to his faith in God and relied on supernatural strength en route to a divine purpose. He was even reconciled back to a right relationship with his brothers (see Genesis 45). Just like Dave Dravecky, Joseph persevered through intense trials and came out on the other side victorious.

While Joseph faced a much different set of trials than Dave, both men trusted God even in the face of turmoil and tragedy. And because of that unwavering faith, they discovered the fullness of His plan and the truth behind this invaluable biblical principle:

"...we also glory in our sufferings, because we know that suffering produces perseverance; perseverance, character; and character, hope." – Romans 5:3-4

The Apostle Paul's words are reminiscent of the German philosopher Friedrich Nietzsche's famous phrase: "That which does not kill us makes us stronger." There's no doubt, we will all go through hard times–some harder than others. It might be a financial crisis, the loss of a loved one, a debilitating disease, an emotional breakdown or a heartbreaking rejection. But for those who trust in God, there is access to His grace, which gives us the strength to persevere. Over time, that perseverance builds up our character and fortifies our resolve. We can then truly experience these words written by David:

"Even though I walk through the darkest valley, I will fear no evil, for you are with me." - Psalm 23:4a

Whether in the middle of our most difficult trial or during a time of peace and tranquility, we can see beyond any circumstance and recognize that we have hope and a future that God has prepared for us, both here in this world and in the world to come. – *CB*

Life Long Lesson
When you're going through tough times in your life, remember that God turns defeats into victories.

Going Long

1. Have you personally fought through a physical battle like Dave Dravecky did or do you know someone else who has? What was the most difficult challenge that you had to overcome during that situation?

2. What are some other personal challenges that have tested your character and your will to persevere? What were some of the things that helped get you through the toughest times?

3. Read Romans 5:3-4. Take each part of that verse (suffering pro-

duces perseverance, perseverance produces character, character produces hope) and apply them to a situation you've faced or something you are currently facing. Can you see where each part of that chain fits together in your story or are there parts with which you're still struggling to embrace?

4. Read Psalm 23 (the entire chapter). What are some portions of this scripture that encourage you and why?

5. What are some "sufferings" (both in your life and in the lives of those you care most about) in which you need to "glory?" What can you start doing today that will help get you started on a journey of perseverance that will produce character and reveal hope?

Today's Prayer: Lord, help me understand the purpose behind the hard things in life that I must face. Give me Your supernatural strength to persevere and develop the kind of character that will allow me to overcome even greater challenges in the future. I trust You and recognize that You are in control—even when I can't yet see the end of this difficult road.

CHAPTER SIXTEEN

A FIRM HANDSHAKE
Godly Training Starts In the Home

"Train a child in the way he should go, and when he is old he will not turn from it." – Proverbs 22:6 (NIV)

Sometimes greatness can be found in unexpected places.

For 12 years, I spoke annually to the FCA group at Daniels Middle School in Raleigh at the invitation of my close friend Jim Branch who was then the adult volunteer. When you're speaking to a group of kids, sometimes it's easy to see their youth and overlook the great potential in each of them.

But on one particular night in 1998, I met a special young man. When Jim introduced us, it didn't take long to see that there was something different about him. At the age of 13, he was already regarded as one of the best teenage golfers in the state of North Carolina. That's not what stood out to me. He gave me a firm handshake and looked me right in the eyes when we spoke. I lost count of how many times he said, "Yes sir."

When I got home that evening, I did something I'd never done before. I called his father Sam and asked him to put the boy's mother Debbie on the other line. I told them how impressed I was with their son during our short conversation. It was obvious to me that these parents had done an excellent job raising their child with godly training and prayerful instruction.

In 2012, the young man returned to Raleigh as the featured speaker at the FCA Spring Banquet. Now a 27-year old husband and father, he shared the following Bible verse:

"Consider it pure joy, my brothers and sisters, whenever you face tri-als of many kinds, because you know that the testing of your faith produces perseverance." – James 1:2-3

He had experienced some of those trials during the early stages of his career on the PGA Tour. He stood by his best friend who while serving as his caddy battled a minor physical disorder and eventually had to step away from the bag. Webb was overjoyed, however, when he learned that his friend intended to become involved with full time Christian ministry.

His parents were at the banquet and I reminded them of our conversation from 14 years earlier. We had a good time discussing it again. A few months later, this same young man won the U.S. Open. Yes, it was Webb Simpson.

Shortly after the momentous occasion, I wrote Sam Simpson a letter. It simply said, "Congratulations! And to think it happened on Father's Day. I know you were a nervous wreck because I was a nervous wreck and he isn't even my son."

Yes, it was just a coincidence that I met Webb as a young middle school student and reconnected with the championship golfer and his family through FCA. – *AL*

Godly Training Starts In The Home

By the time Albert met young Webb, he had already raised three adult sons of his own—Mike, Kirk and Danny. Albert fully recognized the challenges of bringing up respectful, godly young people in a world system that seeks to indoctrinate our youth with contradictory values. Perhaps that's why Webb stood out.

So it was no surprise for Albert to learn that Webb's Christian upbringing had set the tone for the kind of husband, father and competitor he is today. Webb exhibits the same godly characteristics as other athletes like Tim Tebow, Jeremy Lin, Josh Hamilton and Jonathan Byrd–all of which share similar family backgrounds. In the Gospel of Luke, we read about a man known as John the Baptist. Considered by many scholars to be Jesus' cousin, he was a passionate preacher and prophet who compelled the people to repent of their sins and prepare for the coming Messiah. But sometimes it's easy to forget that John's parents were actually the catalysts for one of history's most powerful evangelistic ministries. His father Zacharias was a faithful priest and his mother Elisabeth too was known to be a godly woman. Luke describes them this way:

"Both of them were righteous in the sight of God, observing all the Lord's commands and decrees blamelessly." – Luke 1:6 (NIV)

Following his parents' example and learning from their teaching of the Scriptures, John famously baptized Jesus and later was imprisoned and eventually beheaded for speaking out against King Herod's sinful ways. Today, John is considered one of the preeminent heroes of the Christian faith. Surely, Zacharias and Elisabeth had raised their son under the admonition of King Solomon's teachings:

"Train a child in the way he should go, and when he is old he will not turn from it." – Proverbs 22:6 (NIV)

Living by this principle doesn't mean our children will be perfect. We live in a fallen world and therefore our children will make mistakes and will sometimes even turn away from the training they received as youth. But if the seed of truth has been planted in their hearts, it will eventually bear fruit and point them back towards their parents' faith.

Here are some important questions that we as parents (not to mention grandparents and extended family members) need to ask:

- Are we creating an environment in our homes that not only teaches by example but also models godliness?

- Are we protecting our children from outside influences that seek to turn them away from God?

- Are we preparing our children for the challenges that they will face in their schools and eventually in their lives outside of the home?

If the answer to those questions is "yes," than keep fighting the good fight on behalf of these young people that are precious in God's sight. If you're not sure, then study what the Bible has to say about parenting and prayerfully ask the Lord to guide your steps. – *CB*

Going Long

Life Long Lesson
Godly training starts in the home and follows a child for the rest of their life.

1. Have you ever had a child in your life (as a parent, grandparent, uncle, aunt, etc.) that had an impact on you?

2. In what ways do you think Zacharias and Elisabeth's parenting influenced John the Baptist's ministry?

3. Read Proverbs 22:6. Have you ever seen this verse manifested in the life of someone you know? Why do you think parental guidance is so important for our children?

4. Read Proverbs 29:15-17 and Ephesians 6:4. What do these scrip-

tures have to say about the right way and the wrong way to raise godly children? What are some typical differences in outcome between positive parenting and negative parenting?

5. What are some things that you can do today that will help you become a better parent, grandparent or individual that has influence over children?

Today's Prayer: Lord, help me to take my responsibility as a role model and positive influence in the lives of children seriously and soberly. Give me the wisdom to teach them Your ways. Give me the strength to exercise consistent discipline. Give me the grace to walk out my relationship with You as a living example.

CHAPTER SEVENTEEN

PISTOL PETE
God Turns Your Loss Into Gain

"Yet indeed I also count all things loss for the excellence of the knowledge of Christ Jesus my Lord, for whom I have suffered the loss of all things, and count them as rubbish, that I may gain Christ and be found in Him." – Philippians 3:8-9a (NKJV)

It doesn't add up in the natural, but in God's economy, it's quite possible to lose something and still win. As far as I'm concerned, "Pistol Pete" Maravich is one of the best examples of that biblical principle.

Pete was one of the greatest NCAA basketball players to ever play the game. He was a three-time All-American and the 1970 AP Player of the Year. In four years at LSU, he averaged 44 points a game, but as a long-range shooter, it was later determined that Pete would have averaged 57 points a game if he had played with a three-point line!

The Atlanta Hawks selected Pete with the third pick of the 1970 NBA Draft. He played in the league for 10 years and made five All-Star Teams. But the last few years of his career were marred by knee problems and he was forced to retire in 1980.

Pete had everything the world could offer but when basketball was taken away, he struggled to find significance in his life. He became a recluse and turned to every religion and philosophy imaginable. Then Pete found Jesus and his life was changed.

It was about 1984 when John Lotz introduced me to Pete. Two years later, in November of 1986, the three of us were together with Lester Matte for a youth rally in Lexington, North Carolina. Earlier that afternoon, Pete spoke at Duke University before a football

Pete Maravich holding a copy of his book *Heir To A Dream*. He was one of God's great servants before his death in 1998.

game to over 15,000 young people. He told them about his new relationship with Jesus Christ. The crowd listened to every word Pete had to say.

On our way up to Lexington, he couldn't stop talking. But the conversation wasn't about basketball. It was all about his new life with the Lord. When we got to the high school auditorium, the gathering was much smaller with about 250 people present. I served as the emcee, Lester did his karate demonstration and John gave a brief testimony before introducing Pete who was the special guest speaker.

Pete spoke for a long time but everyone listened, not because of who he was, but because of what he had to say. You could see the sincerity all over him. It was obvious that you were listening to a modern day miracle.

As Pete concluded, there was an invitation given and about a dozen people responded to go with him to another room for counseling and prayer.

As they departed I was clearly led to continue with the invitation. I used an illustration that had been very effective over the past several years. I took off my Rolex watch, showed it to the crowd and explained how many in the audience were just like that watch. They were beautiful on the outside, but fake on the inside. I reminded them that they could not fool God and asked anyone who wanted to be real for Christ needed to get up and join the others in the counseling room. That was it. There wasn't even any singing. It was quite simple and right to the point. Over two dozen young people responded to that spontaneous invitation.

On the way back home that night, Pete again was very talkative. Just like before, it wasn't about basketball, but this time it was about what had happened in that high school auditorium. He kept asking me how I gave the invitation and to tell him about the watch. I explained to Pete that I had done nothing. The Holy Spirit had directed everything. I did not understand it, nor could I explain it.

Pete was so excited to hear that the counselors would follow up with everyone who made decisions for Christ that night. He was just one of four men that had sowed seeds. There was no NBA championship ring awarded or any recognition for what happened. There was probably nothing in the local paper that next day. But this one thing I do know. Our Lord was pleased.

A few months later, Pete was inducted into Basketball Hall of Fame. Early that next year, on January 5, 1998, he died at the age of 40 from heart failure while playing in a pickup basketball game. Pete was out in Pasadena to tape a segment for James Dobson's Focus on the Family radio show that aired later that day.

An autopsy revealed that Pete died of a rare congenital heart defect. He had been born with a missing left coronary artery. It turns out that Pete was a modern day miracle in more ways than one. Nobody with that heart condition had ever lived past the age of 20. You read that correctly—nobody. It seemed appropriate that John Lotz and Dr. Dobson eulogized him at this funeral in Baton Rouge, Louisiana.

It was just a coincidence that John introduced me to Pete Maravich over 30 years ago. I'm so thankful that I was able to see first-hand a remarkable example of how someone can lose something and still win. As it says in Philippians 3:8-9, Pete "suffered the loss of all things," but was able to "gain Christ and be found in Him." – *AL*

God Turns Your Loss Into Gain

Saul was the greatest persecutor of Christians who ever lived. Then he met Jesus on the road to Damascus and his life was changed forever. He changed his name to Paul and began a new journey as one of the greatest evangelists in the history of the Christian faith.

So what changed?

In Philippians 3:8-9a, Paul explains it this way:

"Yet indeed I also count all things loss for the excellence of the knowledge of Christ Jesus my Lord, for whom I have suffered the loss of all things, and count them as rubbish, that I may gain Christ and be found in Him." (NKJV)

Pete Maravich wasn't a mean, vindictive person before he came to Christ, but like Saul, he had absolutely nothing to do with God and His spiritual principles. Then when he met Jesus, just like Paul, you could not hold him back. Pete talked about his relationship with Jesus to everyone wherever we went. He never compromised his faith in Christ regardless of the situation he faced.

It took losing basketball for Pete to find true purpose in life. He found "the excellence of the knowledge of Christ Jesus" his Lord. And then when he left this world so suddenly at the age of 40, Pete was able to fully understand the meaning of something else Paul wrote:

"For to me, to live is Christ and to die is gain." – Philippians 1:21 (NIV). – AL

> **Life Long Lesson**
> **When you're fearful of giving your life to Christ,**
> **remember that God turns your loss into gain.**

Going Long

1. In this story, we read about how Pete Maravich didn't find true purpose and fulfillment until he lost something that he held dear. Can you think of other examples where losing something might help someone find something even better?

2. Go back and read Philippians 3:8-9a. Why do you think Paul was able to write so passionately about suffering for the cause of Christ? Have you ever had to suffer or lose something because of your faith?

3. What are some things that we gain when we enter into a relationship with Jesus Christ?

4. Read Philippians 1:21. What do you think Paul means when he writes, "to live is Christ?" What do you think he means by the phrase, "to die is gain?"

5. What are some ways that you can start living with the same attitude that the Apostle Paul conveyed in those passages and that Pete Maravich displayed late in his life?

Today's Prayer: Lord, transform my way of thinking from a temporal, materialistic mindset that places comfort and short-term benefits in front of eternal things. Help me embrace the principle of living for Jesus in this life while at the same time longing for the time when I will forever be with You in the next life.

CHAPTER EIGHTEEN

Country Bumpkin, God Sees Beneath The Surface

"The Lord does not look at the things people look at. People look at the outward appearance, but the Lord looks at the heart." - 1 Samuel 16:7b (NIV)

"Never judge a book by its cover."

We've heard that old phrase time and time again, but sometimes we just can't help ourselves. We see someone that stands out because of the way they look and we make up our mind about what kind of person they must be.

I have to admit, that's happened to me a time or two. Back in the mid-80s, I was speaking at an FCA function in Concord. This particular event included a meal and I was enjoying some of that delicious western North Carolina barbeque. Yes, there is a difference between western and eastern barbeque in North Carolina where they make the best anywhere in the country.

While sitting at a table by myself, a man asked if he could join me. He looked like a "country bumpkin" with his hunting cap, hunting jacket and hunting boots. I just knew his name was going to be Bubba or Clem or Zeke. I was wrong about that and everything else too. This man was sharp as a tack and I was determined to learn more about him.

I'm so glad that I did.

I found out that he was a successful businessman in Mount Pleasant, NC. A year or so later, he became a board member of my ministry Happenings, Inc. In 1996, he was the Republican nominee for governor and he served North Carolina's 8th congressional district in the U.S. House of Representatives from 1999 to 2009. After that, he became the chairman of the North Carolina Republican Party in 2011.

Yes, it was just a coincidence that the good Lord sent Robin Hayes over to sit next to me at that FCA event. To this day, I've never met a more intelligent man and he and his wife Barbara are two of the most committed Christians I've been blessed to call my friends.

"Never judge a book by its cover."

I guarantee you that I never have since. – *AL*

God Sees Beneath The Surface

Albert shouldn't feel too bad about caving in to his human nature when he met Robin Hayes. We all pass judgment on people based on first impressions whether our thoughts are positive, negative or neutral. It's been that way since the fall of man.

In Old Testament times, another man of God was warned not to do the same thing. His name was Samuel and he was the last Hebrew judge and the first of Israel's major prophets. The Israelites were clamoring for a king and even though this was not what God had designed for His people, He gave them what they wanted.

God told Samuel to anoint an animal herder named Saul to be the first king. He looked the part, but his reign ultimately was a failure. While Saul was still on the throne, God commanded Samuel to anoint his successor (1 Samuel 16). He sent Samuel to visit a man named Jesse who had eight sons. Each one of the oldest seven sons appeared to be fine candidates to take Saul's place, but God had given this word of admonition:

"The Lord does not look at the things people look at. People look at

the outward appearance, but the Lord looks at the heart." – 1 Samuel 16:7b (NIV)

Samuel asked to see the remaining son, a shepherd boy named David, and immediately knew he was the one that God had chosen. Even though he was the youngest and not the obvious choice, the Lord knew that he had the heart of a courageous warrior and strong leader.

It's a good thing that God doesn't determine our destiny based on exterior factors. Otherwise, there's no telling how many amazing people might have been disqualified from doing great things. So the next time you're tempted to judge someone based on their outward appearance, remember that God looks on the inside and sees the possibility within everyone– *CB*

Life Long Lesson
Despite what our human eyes tell us, remember that God sees beneath the surface and looks at the heart.

Going Long

1. Like Albert, have you ever developed preconceived ideas about a person based on their outward appearance? Can you give an example?

2. What are some ways that we tend to judge others based on that standard?

3. Have you ever found out that your ideas about a person were very different from reality? Explain.

4. What are some other ways that looks can be deceiving?

5. Read 1 Samuel 16:7. Why do you think God made sure to

instruct Samuel to discern between physical appearance and the contents of one's heart?

6. How might getting to know people and finding out what's beneath the surface change the way you approach relationships and personal encounters in the future?

Today's Prayer: Lord, help me not to judge people with my natural eyes. Help me instead to see others with Your eyes. Help me take the time to get to know those that I encounter for who they are on the inside so that I won't miss out on an opportunity to befriend them, love them, serve them and minister the Gospel to them.

CHAPTER NINETEEN

THE STRAIGHT AND NARROW
God Leads The Righteous

"He leads me in the paths of righteousness for His name's sake." –
Psalm 23:3 (NKJV)

Integrity is an adherence to a code of values, and people that live with godly integrity can be assured that the Lord will direct their paths.

I have never known any person who walked that straight and narrow road like Clyde King. I could write an entire book on what Clyde meant to me during 35 years or so that we were friends. I learned so much from him and was grateful to have him serve on the Happenings Board of Directors for 20 years.

Clyde was a star pitcher at the University of North Carolina and spent seven years in the Major Leagues with the Brooklyn Dodgers and the Cincinnati Reds. He managed several minor league teams before working his way to jobs with San Francisco and Atlanta. It's amazing to realize that Clyde managed Willie Mays and Willie McCovey in San Francisco and Hank Aaron during his one season with the Braves.

But Clyde was best known for his lengthy time spent in New York's front office where he spent 30 of his 60 years in baseball as a scout, pitching coach, general manager and special advisor to the legendary Yankees owner George Steinbrenner. Clyde was in baseball for an astounding seven decades. I doubt anyone will ever break that record.

Jackie and I always looked forward to going with Clyde and his wife Norma to Bob Bryan's beach home at Morehead City each summer. It was there that I always looked forward to hearing Clyde tell some of Yogi Berra's old jokes. Regardless of how many times I heard them, I laughed harder and harder each time.

I also remember how he would often show one of his seven World Series rings to different people he met. But it wasn't to boast about it his accomplishments. Instead, he would let them know that those rings were nothing compared to his personal relationship with Jesus Christ.

One of the greatest honors I have ever had was when Norma (whom I still call my "second mama") called to ask me to be a pallbearer at his funeral in November of 2010. I think the only person that was more excited about that than me was David Hartman, the first host of "Good Morning America." He and Clyde were very close because of David's love of baseball and their association throughout Clyde's career.

It was just a coincidence that God put Clyde King in my life. He was a very special man, and what a privilege it was to be his friend. Clyde taught me a very important lesson, but it wasn't through a sermon or a conversation. I learned that God orders the steps of the righteous through Clyde's example as someone who never compromised his faith in Jesus Christ regardless of the situation. – *AL*

God Leads The Righteous

In the Old Testament, integrity was often used to describe righteousness or right living. There were many great examples of godly integrity such as Abraham, Joseph and Daniel. All of these men had something in common. While not perfect, they did their best to follow the path that God had paved for them to walk. And because of their faithfulness, God always took care of them, even in times of great trouble.

During his 84 years of life, Clyde King was also a great example of godly integrity. He understood and followed the command that Jesus gave His disciples regarding righteous living:

"Enter through the narrow gate. For wide is the gate and broad is the road that leads to destruction, and many enter through it. But small is the gate and narrow the road that leads to life, and only a few find it." – Matthew 7:13-14 (NIV)

Jesus was telling His disciples three things here:

1) He was reminding them that doing the right things and living according to His standard is not the easy way to go. Making good choices can be difficult and contrary to the world's way of thinking.
2) Jesus was warning them about the destructive future that awaits those who reject godly integrity, both in this life and in eternity.
3) He was encouraging them to that although it's a more difficult path, the life of righteousness leads to abundant life on earth and eternal life in heaven.

God has a path of integrity that He wants each of us to follow. And when we walk on that path, we gain favor, protection and abundant life, just like Clyde did during his more than 60 years in baseball over seven decades. And we will then begin to understand the truth behind these powerful words written by King David:

"The LORD directs the steps of the godly. He delights in every detail of their lives." – Psalm 37:23 (NLT) – CB

Life Long Lesson
God leads the righteous to an abundant life in Him.

Going Long

1. How do you think the world would describe "a righteous man?" Is that description the same or different than God's description?

2. Why is integrity such a difficult thing for people to maintain in today's society? What are some things that challenge our integrity? Which of those things do you personally struggle against?

3. Read Matthew 7:13-14. Go through each part of this verse and break down the lessons that Jesus is teaching us about integrity and consequences.

4. How might we be rewarded for living with integrity here on earth? What are some consequences that might arise from living without integrity? How does those rewards and consequences transfer over into the eternal realm?

5. Read Psalm 37:23. What are some specific ways that the Lord directs the steps of the godly? Have you experienced His direction, favor, protection, etc.? How significant is it to you that God delights in every detail of your life?

6. What are some things you can start doing today that will help you become more vigilant in your efforts to live with godly integrity?

Today's Prayer: Lord, reveal to me areas where I am not living with godly integrity and then guide me back to the path that you have paved for me. I want to make right choices and walk the straight and narrow road that will bring abundant life here on earth and eternally in heaven.

CHAPTER TWENTY

CAT'S IN THE CRADLE
Godly Fathers Put Family First

"But as for me and my household, we will serve the LORD." –
Joshua 24:15b (NIV)

In today's day and age, the role of the father has been diminished. Even worse, some men are abdicating their responsibilities in the home. I'm thankful that I had great examples of godly fatherhood including my good friend John West.

John isn't a professional comedian, but he is one of the funniest men I have ever known. He once served as Furman University's athletic director and later spent 15 years as an associate pastor at Prestonwood Baptist Church in Dallas, Texas.

I met John through FCA for whom he would often speak at summer conferences held in Black Mountain, North Carolina and Rome, Georgia. He was always there with his wife Charlotte. During his days at Furman, John was always gracious to invite our team members to speak at the school's FCA meeting. It was also at Furman's FCA where I was blessed to meet award-winning recording artist Amy Grant who roomed with John's daughter there.

Going to the mall with John was always quite an experience. He loved to talk to mannequins. John would walk up to one and start a humorous conversation. You wouldn't believe how that would draw a crowd.

But John's real gift was public speaking. He spoke often during the evening as the primary guest at many FCA events. His trademark was reciting the words from Harry Chapin's hit song "Cat's In The Cradle."

In that iconic 1974 chart topping hit "Cat's In The Cradle," Harry Chapin sings from the perspective of a father who is too busy with his work to spend quality time with his son. By the time the son becomes a man, the aging father finds that his boy has tragically grown up to be just like him.

It was very important for John to teach the fathers in the crowd the importance of being actively involved in their children's lives.

John is retired now and lives in Travelers Rest, SC where he helps fundraise for North Greenville University. His greatest gift to me, however, will always be the lingering message he conveyed about what it means to be a godly father. I'm so thankful that the good Lord arranged another coincidence and put me together with John West. – *AL*

Godly Fathers Put Family First

Harry Chapin's lyrics in the song "Cat's In The Cradle" offer a cautionary tale for modern day fathers that find themselves busy trying to provide for their families or even to those serving in the ministry. But according to God's Word, a successful father will understand that his most important job is to be his family's spiritual leader. Here are four things that the Bible tells how godly fathers are engaged in their children's lives:

1. Fathers are compassionate: We should show the same kind of love for our children as God shows for *His* children. (Psalm 103:13)

2. Fathers are teachers: One of the greatest ways a father can stay actively involved in his child's life is through biblically inspired instruction in the same way that Moses advised the Israelites when he gathered them to share the Ten Commandments. (Deuteronomy 6:6-7)

3. Fathers are disciplinarians: Correction is one of the most difficult aspects of fathering, but is also one of the most important. Without it, children are left directionless and lacking in the necessary skills to make good decisions. (Proverbs 13:24)

4. Fathers are leaders: The most powerful way a father can stay involved in his children's lives is to actively lead them in both word and deed. A father's example is his most effective tool. (Joshua 24:15b)

We too face the same choice. Will we fall in the world's trap as unengaged fathers that chase worldly success or will we follow God's example as a father who loves, teaches, disciplines and leads His children? Our decision could have an eternally significant impact. – *CB*

Life Long Lesson
Godly fathers put family first through acts of
compassion, teaching, discipline and leadership.

Going Long

1. What have you personally observed about the diminishing influence of fathers in today's society? To what do you attribute this troubling trend?

2. What are some ways that fathers can get distracted from their responsibilities in the home? Have you ever dealt with those kinds of distractions? If so, how did you handle them?

3. What are some of the important roles that a father should be

playing in his children's lives? How would you rank those roles from most important to least important?

4. Go through the four areas discussed in the devotional (compassionate, teacher, disciplinarian and leader) and read the accompanying scriptures. Which of these four do you personally find most difficult? How does God's Word challenge you to do a better job in that area?

5. What are some things that you can start to do today to be a more actively involved father or (for those who aren't yet fathers) prepare for fatherhood or perhaps apply these principles to mentor a fatherless child?

Today's Prayer: Lord, fill my heart with compassion and concern for my children. Give me wisdom to better manage my time so that I might fulfill all of my responsibilities as a provider, teacher, disciplinarian, spiritual guide and godly example. Open the door for other opportunities to serve and mentor children who might not have a father actively involved in their lives.

CHAPTER TWENTY-ONE

PRAYER LIST
God Hears Our Intercessions

"With this in mind, be alert and always keep on praying for all the Lord's people." – Ephesians 6:18b (NIV)

Targeted prayer is a must within the Body of Christ.

I first learned about the importance of having a daily prayer list from Steve Robinson. He is the Fellowship of Christian Athletes Director for Middle Tennessee and, along with my good friend Doug Scott, has worked for the organization longer than just about anyone I know. Because of Steve's advice, I pray for about 15 people each day of the week instead of putting a needle on a record for so many people at one time. This way you can most certainly concentrate on fewer people, which is so important.

Praying specifically for individuals and concentrating on each as you are praying for them is so important. I read the following in David Jeremiah's book on prayer:

Prayer changes us. Prayer doesn't change God. When we pray, we get on the same wavelength with God. And as we pray, and if we pray according to the will of God, little by little He takes all the things that are out of sync in our lives and puts them into sync so we can take this big deep breath and say "Oh yes, that's the way it is supposed to be! Your will be done on earth."

Jeremiah also said something in another message about prayer that impacted my prayer life. He explained that Jesus taught us to begin and end our prayer with praise. When we finish praying, we remind ourselves that God is sovereign, that He is powerful, that He is majestic, and that He is forever. That's what I always try and incorporate with my daily prayer list.

Raymond Berry is one of the people that I have frequently had on my prayer list. There is no doubt in my mind that he was the greatest receiver in Baltimore Colts history. Raymond played on Baltimore's two NFL Championship teams and was inducted into the Pro Football Hall of Fame. He also spent several years as an NFL coach and led the New England Patriots to the franchise's first Super Bowl appearance (Super Bowl XX) during the 1985 season.

I first met Raymond and his wife Sally at an FCA conference at Black Mountain. We still remain good friends today and stay in touch with each other occasionally. I've truly enjoyed getting to know such a great man of God.

When his picture appeared on the cover of FCA's *Sharing The Victory* magazine, I sent it to him and asked him to autograph it for me. It hangs on a special place in my study. Later, I wrote him a letter to let him know that I was still praying for him and his family each Thursday. I got a special note back from him that I placed right under his picture. It reads, "Hi Albert. Thanks for your intercession. That is the only way I make it."

It was just a coincidence that the good Lord put us together and taught me an important lesson about praying for our brothers and sisters in Christ. – *AL*

God Hears Our Intercessions

When Albert prays for the people on his daily list, not only does God *hear* his intercessions, He *responds* by blessing those individuals with such spiritual gifts as strength, peace and joy.

In the Old Testament, David wrote often how our God hears our prayers:

"The righteous cry out, and the Lord hears them..." – *Psalm 34:17a (NIV)*

Then, in the New Testament, the Apostle James affirms that the Father answers prayers and intervenes on behalf of our intercessions:

"The prayer of a righteous person has great power as it is working."
– James 5:16b (NIV)

There is even greater power in those two concepts when we apply them to the charge we have been given in Ephesians 6:18 by the Apostle Paul who encourages us to take the needs of our fellow Christians to God in prayer:

"With this in mind, be alert and always keep on praying for all the Lord's people." – Ephesians 6:18b (NIV)

Raymond Berry provided Albert with real proof that praying for others brings real results. He could attest to the fact that people were interceding on his behalf because God's strength was present in his life. Just as we would hope to have other praying for us on a regular basis, we too should take the time to lift others up in order to help them make it through life's difficult moments. – *CB*

Going Long

Life Long Lesson
God hears our intercessions and responds.

1. What does the word "intercession" mean to you? How is it the same and/or different from the word "prayer?"

2. Why do you think it's important for us to pray for fellow Christians?

3. How have you personally benefited from the prayers of other Christians? Have you ever learned that your prayers blessed someone else?

4. Read Ephesians 6:18. Why do you think Paul says that we should "be alert" in relation to our prayers for others?

5. Who are some people that God has laid on your heart recently? Make up a daily prayer list and commit to interceding for those individuals.

Today's Prayer: Lord, place people on my heart that could benefit from prayerful intercession. Give me a burden that will consistently remind me to take time away from my busy schedule. I want to be a blessing to my fellow Christian brethren by seeking Your face on their behalf.

CHAPTER TWENTY-TWO

THE WORLD IS MINE
God Satisfies The Thankful Heart

"Let them give thanks to the Lord for his unfailing love and his wonderful deeds for mankind, for he satisfies the thirsty and fills the hungry with good things." – Psalm 107:8-9

Sometimes it can be easy to take things for granted. It can be even easier to find reasons to complain. But God will always satisfy, fulfill and bless those who have a thankful heart.

Mike O'Koren has always been a great example of that truth. He is one of my all-time favorite UNC basketball players along with Phil Ford and Charlie Scott (who are the only two people I know that still call me "Mr. Long") and my two Christian brothers Bobby Jones and Al Wood who were both incredible NBA players that have meant so much to me spiritually.

Mike played for the Tar Heels from 1976 to 1980 and was twice named a Second Team All-American. After his senior year, he traveled with the Happening team on three different occasions. The place was packed every time he was scheduled to speak. It's amazing how athletes could draw a crowd back then just like they do today.

Mike went on to play eight years in the NBA with the New Jersey Nets and the Washington Bullets. He then spent seven seasons coaching at both New Jersey and Washington. Mike grew up in a tough neighborhood of Jersey City called the Heights. That's why he was always so effective when ministering to inner city kids. He could relate to them in a very personal way.

I think that's why Mike loved the poem "The World Is Mine"

so much. It was a poem that I used at every high school assembly and sports banquet at which I spoke. He would always comment about what the poem meant to him every time he heard me share it. Mike also read it on numerous occasions when speaking to youth audiences during his NBA career. It reminded him to be thankful no matter what and to never take his blessings for granted.

In the poem, written by Joy Lovelet Crawford, there are three scenes that depict individuals dealing with difficult physical problems. One character struggles to walk, one is blind, and the other is deaf. In the end, the writer comes to this sobering conclusion:

> *With feet to take me where I would go*
> *With eyes to see the sunsets glow*
> *With ears to hear what I would know*
> *O God forgive me when I whine*
> *I'm blessed, indeed, the world is mine.*

After reading the poem, I would always tell the audience to "always remember that he or she who is healthy is rich, but doesn't realize it."

I'm so glad the Lord arranged such a wonderful coincidence that allowed me to become close friends with Mike O'Koren, a man who is truly a genuine example of thankfulness. – *AL*

God Satisfies The Thankful Heart

God is pleased when we are thankful. Perhaps this is true because thankfulness so often requires a selfless attitude and a rejection of the pride that easily causes us to stumble. When we are thankful, we are telling God that we trust Him and that we are grateful for His blessings–even in times when we don't get exactly what we want in life.

And the good news is that when we are thankful, God is faithful to take care of our physical, emotional and spiritual needs just as David recognized in his writings:

"Let them give thanks to the Lord for his unfailing love and his wonderful deeds for mankind, for he satisfies the thirsty and fills the hungry with good things." – Psalm 107:8-9

The Apostle Paul also had a firm grasp of this concept. Even though he went through many trials because of his faith (imprisonment, beatings, banishment, etc), he still managed to find the blessings amid the less than desirable circumstances:

"Give thanks in all circumstances; for this is God's will for you in Christ Jesus." – 1 Thessalonians 5:18 (NIV)

And while it is wise to understand how God "satisfies the thirsty and fills the hungry" of those who are consistently thankful, it's also important to understand the treacherous path walked by those who choose to complain. After being freed from captivity in Egypt, the Israelites were notorious for their unthankful attitudes. Those who complained never saw the Promised Land and some of them even paid the ultimate price.

"And do not grumble, as some of them did–and were killed by the destroying angel." – 1 Corinthians 10:10

On paper, it might seem like an easy decision to choose thankfulness over ingratitude. But our daily lives can take a toll on our spiritual resolve. Like Mike O'Koren, it's always best to take the road less traveled and maintain a sincerely thankful heart no matter what circumstances we face. Then, we can trust God to take care of the rest. – *CB*

Life Long Lesson
When you're tempted to complain,
remember that God satisfies the thankful heart.

Going Long

1. What are some things that people tend to complain about? Can you think of some times when you've caught yourself complaining? How did complaining impact your situation?

2. What are some things that you are thankful for? What do you tend to spend more doing, complaining or being thankful?

3. Why does it seem easier for people to complain than to be thankful?

4. Read Psalm 107:8-9. What does this verse mean to you? Have you ever experienced the satisfaction described by David? Explain.

5. Read 1 Corinthians 10:1-10. In this passage, Paul is recounting the troubles that God's people faced when they disobeyed Him and complained about their circumstances after being freed from slavery in Egypt. How would you relate this story to modern times? Have you seen or personally experienced a situation where complaining made things worse?

6. Take some time to write out things for which you are most thankful. What are some other ways that you can be intentional in your effort to give thanks on a daily basis?

Today's Prayer: Lord, create in me a heart that is thankful in both good and bad times. Help me resist the temptation to complain when things don't go my way. Satisfy my soul in a way that only You can.

CHAPTER TWENTY-THREE

CIRCLE OF INFLUENCE
God Pours Favor On The Faithful

"A faithful man will be richly blessed." – Proverbs 28:20a (NIV)

Everyone has a circle of influence. Some circles are bigger than others, but what's most important is how we faithfully use that influence to impact our world with the Gospel of Jesus Christ.

I can't think of a better example of a man who faithfully impacted his circle of influence than Nick Hyder.

I had heard all about Nick long before I met him. He was the head football coach at Valdosta High School in Georgia where his program was known as one of the best in the South. In 22 years, he won seven state titles and three national championships. It was no surprise when Nick was inducted into the Georgia Sports Hall of Fame in 1997 and into the second class of the Georgia Athletic Coaches Association Hall of Fame in 2002.

My friendship with Nick began like so many others at Black Mountain where we were both attending an FCA conference. One year while I was there, I took Nick up to visit Dr. Calvin Thielman who was one of my early mentors and a future Advisory Board Member of Happenings, Inc. Calvin was one of my dearest friends and Dr. Billy Graham's pastor in Montreat. After that first year of visitation, Nick never came to Black Mountain unless he grabbed me and said, "Let's go visit Calvin." It was a must for him and I certainly loved being around those two guys. Calvin even invited him to come to Montreat and speak at chapel.

Many years later Nick was the chairman for our "Happening" in Valdosta. He was a one-man team and really blessed all of us that came to minister. Each December he would send me a $100 bill with the same message. "Take Jackie out for a very nice meal. Tell Randy, Donna, and Mark that I think about them every time I listen to 'Ten Thousand Joys.'"

In May of 1996, I arrived at my home after being away for a few days. There were four messages on my answering machine telling me the tragic news. Nick had died after suffering a heart attack in the high school cafeteria. I immediately began to cry when I heard that my good friend was gone.

Thousands of people crowded into Bazemore-Hyder Stadium in Valdosta for Nick's funeral. That afternoon, many of his former players shared what he meant to them. Nick was so loved by so many. Winning football games certainly had something to do with that, but it was really because of the kind of man Nick was in the community. He did so much for his hometown and was an inspiration to the young men who played for him all those years.

It was just a coincidence that the good Lord allowed me to meet Nick at Black Mountain and become a part of his circle of influence. His example of faithfulness reminds me how important it is to have a positive impact on those in *my* circle of influence. *– AL*

God Pours Favor On The Faithful

It's doubtful that anyone in Valdosta was shocked when thousands of people showed up for Nick Hyder's memorial service. After all, he had faithfully served in the community for over 20 years and did so with God-centered motives. King Solomon had something interesting to say about men like Nick:

"The memory of the righteous will be a blessing…" – Proverbs 10:7a (NIV)

Certainly that was evident in the outpour of love that Nick's family must have felt in that stadium back in 1996. That's because faithful men and women that serve God are recipients of His favor and as Solomon later writes in Proverbs 28:20a, they "will be richly blessed." (NIV)

But there is more to being faithful than just gaining God's blessings. In fact, it's really more about gaining favor with others and seeing one's circle of influence expanded. Nick, for instance, was faithful as a young high school coach and over time was able to make a significant impact on an entire town.

The Bible gives us several examples of faithful men and women who saw their circles of influence grow exponentially. Joseph, Esther, David and Daniel are just a few Old Testament heroes that experienced such a phenomenon in their lives. And then there's a lesser known Bible figure named Jabez who made this now famous plea to God:

"Oh, that you would bless me and enlarge my territory! Let your hand be with me, and keep me from harm so that I will be free from pain." – 1 Chronicles 4:10 (NIV)

The rest of that verse simply says, "And God granted his request." We are left to wonder what that actually ended up looking like. Perhaps it was more land, more resource or more power within the kingdom. But one thing is for sure. If we are faithful like Nick Hyder and these aforementioned men and women of God, we can expect our circle of influence to get bigger.

Then it's up to us to remain faithful and do what we can to impact the people within that circle for the sake of the Gospel. – *CB*

Life Long Lesson
God pours favor on the faithful and
increased their circles of influence.

Going Long

1. What do you think it means to be faithful to God?

2. Read Proverbs 10:7 and Proverbs 28:20. Why do you think faithfulness is important to God? In what ways have you seen God bless others or yourself for being faithful? What do the second halves of those verses tell us about how God deals with people that are unfaithful?

3. How would you describe the concept of the circle of influence? What kinds of people would you say are typically within *your* circle of influence?

4. Read 1 Chronicles 4:10. Based on the fact that God granted this request, what characteristics do you think Jabez exhibited in his life? What are some ways that you would like to see your territory enlarged? What would you do if your circle of influence were to be increased?

5. What are some things that you can start to do today that would help you became a more faithful servant of God?

Today's Prayer: Lord, I want to be faithful with the circle of influence with which you have entrusted me. I desire Your favor on my life and pray that you would enlarge my territory and allow me to impact even more people for the sake of the Gospel of Jesus Christ.

CHAPTER TWENTY-FOUR

THE GREAT PHYSICIAN
God Heals The Broken Heart

*"He heals the brokenhearted and binds up their wounds." – Psalm
147:3 (NIV)*

The heart is an amazing thing and the One who created it is
even more amazing. That truth became very clear in the midst of a
long-awaited opportunity to meet an NFL legend.

I have over 100 treasured pictures hanging on the walls of my
study. The interesting part is that I have personally met the subject
of each photo. For some time, my collection was missing a picture
of legendary Green Bay Packers quarterback Bart Starr. Bart played
16 seasons and led the Packers to championships as the MVP of
Super Bowl I and Super Bowl II. He went on to coach the team for
nine seasons and was eventually inducted into the Pro Football Hall
of Fame.

Many people said they could arrange to get me an autographed
picture from Bart, but I always said, "One day the good Lord will
put us together." And in 1978, the good Lord did.

I was invited to speak at the team's chapel when Green Bay
was playing in Denver. Afterwards, Bart invited me to have breakfast with him. He was such a classy guy and later sent me the picture that is still on my wall today.

But believe it or not, that wasn't even the highlight of my trip.

My dear friend Dr. Fred Schoonmaker, who is now home with
the Lord, invited me to stay with him in Denver and get a thorough
physical while there. Fred was a brilliant cardiologist and the Chief
of Staff at St. Luke's Hospital.

I always like to joke that the physical almost killed me. That might be a slight exaggeration, but what happened next was absolutely incredible. Fred took me into the operating room and allowed me to stand right next to him and observe a heart transplant. Words will never be able to describe that experience. I actually witnessed a modern day miracle.

People often ask me why we don't see the same kind of miracles we read about in the New Testament. I usually answer them by telling them that I can give a few hundred examples of miracles that happen everyday.

It's a miracle every time a baby is born.

It's a miracle that a bumblebee can fly, even though scientists say it should be impossible based on how its body is designed.

It's a miracle how the moon controls the tides.

It's a miracle that a mockingbird can sing over one hundred different songs.

It's a miracle that a tiny hummingbird can migrate across the ocean.

It's a miracle that a person can receive a new heart through a complicated transplant procedure.

Yes, my trip to Denver was a reminder that God still performs miracles and I'm forever indebted to Him for arranging the coincidence that allowed me to enjoy such an incredible experience. – *AL*

God Heals The Broken Heart

The New Testament Gospels are rich with examples of Jesus' miraculous power. He turned water into wine (John 2:1-11), calmed the storms (Mark 4:35-41), walked on water (Matthew 14:22-33), caused the blind to see (John 9:1-12), made the lame walk again (John 5:1-15), cast out demons (Mark 1:21-28) and even raised the dead (John 11:1-44).

But here's the biggest miracle of them all. When Jesus shed His precious blood and gave His life on the cross (Matthew 27:32-56), He made a way for us to be forgiven of our sins and for our relationship with God to be restored. Because He was resurrected three days later (Luke 24:1-12), we now have the promise of eternal life in Heaven.

And the miracle doesn't stop there, when we repent of our sins, we become a new creation (2 Corinthians 5:17). Our lives are transformed and, like that transplant that Albert observed, we receive a brand new heart and our past transgressions are forgiven and forgotten.

Not only does God forgive our sins, but, as David reminds us in the Psalms, He also heals our hurts:

"He heals the brokenhearted and binds up their wounds." – Psalm 147:3

Even after we accept Christ as our Savior, there are still times that we need to accept Him as our Healer or, as He is often called, the Great Physician. And if we don't need healing, there are undoubtedly people in our lives that *do* need a heart transplant or perhaps healing from emotional hurts. In those times, we can pray this prayer for ourselves or for others:

"Heal me, Lord, and I will be healed; save me and I will be saved, for You are the one I praise." – Jeremiah 17:14

Then, it's only a matter of watching God work a miracle in our lives. – *CB*

Life Long Lesson
God heals the broken heart and makes all things new.

Going Long

1. When asked about miracles in the modern age, Albert often responds by mentioning things within the natural and scientific worlds. What are some examples of modern-day miracles that come to your mind?

2. Which of Jesus' miracles do you find to be the most amazing? Why do you think we don't see as many miracles (i.e. physical healings) today?

3. Read 2 Corinthians 5:17. What does that scripture mean to you? Have you experienced this in your life? Explain.

4. Do you view Jesus as "The Great Physician?" If so, how have you seen Him fulfill that role in your life or in the life of others?

5. What are some areas of your heart that need to be healed? What can you do today that will help you accept Jesus as your Healer today?

Today's Prayer: Lord, heal me of my hurts. Renew my heart. Transform my life. And do the same for the people in my life that might be scarred by past sins or pain that has been inflicted upon them by others.

CHAPTER TWENTY-FIVE

THE FOUR SEEDS
God Is Looking For Good Soil

"But the one who received the seed that fell on good soil is the man who hears the word and understands it. He produces a crop, yielding a hundred, sixty or thirty times what was sown." – Matthew 13:23 (NIV)

There is no story in the Bible that describes my salvation experience better than the Parable of the Four Seeds. Jesus shared this illustration while sitting in a boat as a large crowd of people gathered along the shore. The parable went like this:

"A farmer went out to sow his seed. As he was scattering the seed, some fell along the path, and the birds came and ate it up. Some fell on rocky places, where it did not have much soil. It sprang up quickly, because the soil was shallow. But when the sun came up, the plants were scorched, and they withered because they had no root. Other seed fell among thorns, which grew up and choked the plants. Still other seed fell on good soil, where it produced a crop–a hundred, sixty or thirty times what was sown. He who has ears, let him hear."
– Matthew 13:3-9 (NIV)

My full testimony can be found earlier in this book [page 15-16], but to recap, I grew up going to church and was basically a good guy. However, I didn't have my first encounter with the Lord until 1963 at the Fellowship of Christian Athletes conference in Henderson Harbor, NY. When James Jeffrey prayed for me that one evening, I didn't understand what had happened to me. After a month of trying to share my experience with others, I gave up trying and went back to my old way of life.

The next year, I went to my first FCA conference at Black Mountain and "got my battery recharged." This lasted for about five days until I went back home and faced a litany of "don't dos" from several people that I trusted were knowledgeable Christians. It was just too hard, so I decided to go back to sinning because it was a lot more fun and a lot easier to understand.

Another year passed and I was invited to come back to Black Mountain, but this time as a featured speaker. Many of the attendees let me know that I'd done a great job, but one older coach knew something wasn't right. He walked right up to me and put his finger on my nose.

"I've been watching you Long," he said. "I dare you to challenge the resurrection of Jesus Christ. But reject not until you've examined all the evidence."

I asked him to explain the last part of that.

"Challenge that stone," he replied. "Challenge how that stone covered that tomb. Challenge how that stone was moved. Challenge every narrative that was ever written about the resurrected Christ. Every one of them says that the grave clothes remained undisturbed. I dare you to challenge the custodian, those elite soldiers that guarded that tomb."

"But most importantly," he concluded, "I dare you to challenge all of the appearances He made after the resurrection. Then you will really have to decide if He was resurrected or if He wasn't. It has to be one or the other."

That coach challenged me in a way I had not yet been challenged. So I went home and was determined to understand what had happened to me at Henderson Harbor two years earlier. I got involved in a Bible study group and started studying the Word on my own. It wasn't long before I had a powerful encounter with the Lord. He opened my eyes and showed me the truth of what it meant to "believe on" Jesus.

I also began to understand how my experience mirrored the story Jesus told to His followers. He didn't directly explain what that story meant to the masses, but He did share the deeper meaning with His disciples later on:

"Listen then to what the parable of the sower means: When anyone hears the message about the kingdom and does not understand it, the evil one comes and snatches away what was sown in his heart. This is the seed sown along the path. The one who received the seed that fell on rocky places is the man who hears the word and at once receives it with joy. But since he has no root, he lasts only a short time. When trouble or persecution comes because of the word, he quickly falls away. The one who received the seed that fell among the thorns is the man who hears the word, but the worries of this life and the deceitfulness of wealth choke it, making it unfruitful. But the one who received the seed that fell on good soil is the man who hears the word and understands it. He produces a crop, yielding a hundred, sixty or thirty times what was sown." – Matthew 13:18-23

Some people can relate to one, maybe two of these seeds. I can relate to all four.

1. The first seed fell on the path and never even reached the soil. The birds ate up that seed before it could be sown.

That's exactly what I experienced at Henderson Harbor. I heard the Word, but nothing really happened. The Word failed to take root. The enemy of that first seed was Satan. He blinded me from the truth and kept it from ever reaching the soil of my heart.

2. The second seed fell on rocky soil. It might take root and begin to germinate, but because the rock is right below the soil, the roots have no place to go. The plant is beautiful until the sun comes out and then it dries up and dies.

In my story, the second seed was planted in my heart at Black Mountain. There was an explosive growth that year, but no real, lasting conversion. The rejection was as quick as the response because the roots had no place to go. The enemy of that second seed was my flesh.

3. The third seed fell into an area where thorns were present. The seeds began to grow and looked like they were making good progress, but all of a sudden, the thorns choked out the seeds.

This is something I dealt with throughout my story. The thorns represented the pleasures of the world and material gain. If you don't deal with these thorns immediately, you'll be lost. And I was lost. It was still all about me, and what I could get out of life.

4. The fourth seed fell into good soil. This allowed the seed to be cultivated and cared for over time. Before too long, that seed grew into a plant and eventually was able to bear good fruit.

When that coach challenged me to test the Word of God and everything it had to say about the death and resurrection of Jesus Christ, it was like the seed had finally found its way to the good soil. I was ready to receive whatever the Holy Spirit wanted to teach me. The fourth seed was then able to bear fruit from my converted heart.

God Is Looking For Good Soil

Nothing matters until that seed finds its way to the good soil in your heart. Sometimes that soil can be surrounded by thorns or buried beneath a rocky surface. And if you aren't seeking God, often that seed won't even come close to reaching that soil in the first place.

That's what God is searching for. He's looking for that good soil where He can implant His love and His truth in your heart. And once that seed has taken root, you will start to see the fruit in your life just as Jesus explained to His disciples:

"But the one who received the seed that fell on good soil is the man who hears the word and understands it. He produces a crop, yielding a hundred, sixty or thirty times what was sown." – Matthew 13:23 (NIV)

The seed is the Word of God. The soil is the heart.

So how is your heart? Is it hard? Is it shallow? Is it worldly? Or is it understanding. It took me a long, long time in that impossible stage, which is stage number three. It was quick in stage one and quick in stage two, but a long time in stage three. But once I realized that His truth and love was greater than anything the world could offer, the soil of my heart was softened and able to produce fruit.

The first fruit was a greater understanding of His Word. The next fruit was a transformative change in my walk. And from there, the fruit of my relationship with Jesus came in the form of souls that I was able to impact through my testimony.

Early on in my evangelistic work, I was worried to death that the seed wouldn't grow. I thought that *I* was supposed to make it grow. But then the Lord showed me that I *can't* do it. My job wasn't to bring results. My job was to be faithful in teaching the Word of God. The Apostle Paul explained this best when describing his role as an evangelist and his friend Apollos' role as a teacher.

"I planted the seed, Apollos watered it, but God made it grow." – 1 Corinthian 3:6 (NIV)

So again, I ask. How is your fruit? Are you experiencing spiritual growth or are you stagnant and stuck in your old ways? Are you impacting people with the Gospel or are you just going with the flow? Are you like my imitation Rolex watch or are you the real thing? Always remember that you can't fool God!

Allow God to plant that seed deep into the soft soil of your heart and He will use you to do great things for His Kingdom. – *AL*

Going Long

> **Life Long Lesson**
> **God is looking for good soil within the**
> **hearts of all who seek true understanding.**

1. To what parts of Albert's story can you most relate? Which of those four seeds have you personally experienced?

2. What does the story of that first seed mean to you? In what ways can we be blinded to the truth of God's Word?

3. Albert compared the rocky soil from the story of the second seed to a shallow faith that has no roots in God's Word. Have you experienced that reality and if so, what did you do to correct the problem?

4. Thorns choked out the third seed. What are some worldly pleasures or mindsets that might threaten to kill your spiritual growth? How can those things be eradicated from your life?

5. How would you describe "soft soil" within the context of your heart? How does having a soft heart help cultivate understanding and spiritual growth?

6. What kind of fruit do you think a Christian should produce? Are you producing fruit in the areas of understanding, lifestyle change and evangelism? If not, ask the Holy Spirit to soften the soil of your heart and allow true spiritual growth to take root. Be vigilant in those areas and continually check your fruit as your relationship with Jesus strengthens over time.

Today's Prayer: Lord, find any areas in my heart where the soil is hard, shallow or worldly. Soften that soil and make it into fertile ground where Your love, Your truth and Your understanding can take root. I want to produce good fruit. I want to do great things for Your Kingdom.

Psalm 71:18 is my favorite verse of scripture now because it most certainly speaks to me at my age. "Now when I am old and greyheaded, O God, do not forsake me, until I declare your strength to this generation, and Your power to everyone who is to come."